DISTANT FIELDS

THE **AMAZING** CALL OF

GEORGE MARKEY

FROM **FARMLAND** TO **MISSIONS**

WRITTEN BY

JED GOURLEY

JOB 19:24

IRON PEN

BOOKS

DISTANT FIELDS
THE AMAZING CALL OF GEORGE MARKEY FROM FARMLAND TO MISSIONS

by JED GOURLEY

©2014 Jed Gourley

Published by Iron Pen Books

ISBN: 978-0990528708

Cover Design and Internal layout: John Shaffer

Section illustrations by: Oksana Dyachenko

Printed in the U.S.A

for Pam

TABLE OF CONTENTS

FOREWORD

I HAD THE PRIVILEGE of meeting George when I was about 7 years old. Our families are like-minded in many ways and they spent a lot of time together. Not only was George a friend and mentor to my father, but in turn I have been deeply impacted by his life and ministry.

George was one of the most servant-hearted men I have ever met. He never made it seem as though he was making some big sacrifice for ministry; it truly flowed from all of who he was—it just was the way he lived. I remember him working long hours roofing people's houses or doing whatever was needed for anyone who needed help.

One of the things that greatly impacted me was George's heart for the lost. He and my dad were very involved in prison ministry, and I remember countless times going with them and seeing firsthand the importance and reward of leading people to Christ and reaching out to those who need Him. George never shied away from loving those whom other people would perhaps see as unlovable.

George also had an incredible heart for eternity, in all things having an eternal perspective. After the death of my first wife, Melissa, this truth grabbed hold of my heart more than ever before. I can see how the Lord used men like George Markey in my life to sow seeds of what it is to live by faith and to live with our hearts anchored in the hope of heaven.

I hope that as you find this book in your hands, you will be inspired by a life that was fully surrendered to Christ. Of course George was human and made mistakes like all of us, but he was a man of deep compassion and grace from whom we can all learn. A man whose heart was contagiously set on eternity.

Although the Markeys moved to Ukraine when I was still a teenager, their family has had a profound influence on my life. There was a season during high school when I felt that the secular environment was influencing me to my detriment and I needed to go to a Christian school instead. Through George, the Lord provided a car for me to use (because our family could not afford it) so that I could drive to the Christian school, work and clean toilets to pay for my school fees, and grow in my walk with the Lord. This decision most definitely shaped the course of my future because I ended up going to Bible College instead of pursuing football. It was George's generosity and servant's heart that gave me the ability to do what I had to do.

I'm thankful to say that just as my dad ministered alongside George, the Lord has kept the relationship going and I've now had the honor of ministering alongside George's kids. I pray we will all follow his example of laying down our lives for Jesus.

JEREMY CAMP

http://www.speakinglouderministries.com/

http://www.jeremycamp.com/

INTRODUCTION

ALL OF US need examples. We are creatures who learn from observing, studying, and doing. Also, I am convinced that the life stories of each one of us are more integrated than we could ever know, at least this side of heaven. But, getting back to examples... Whether we want to admit it or not, our lives affect one another, and the lives of some people affect us more than those of others.

George Markey was an example to me, to his family, to the members of his congregations, and to practically everyone he met. I have spoken with people who worked side by side with George every day, for years, and who consider him to be the greatest instrument that God used in their lives. I have talked with others who met him only once, yet to this day remember the influence he had on them. And I know of many more who were never acquainted with George personally, but by observing his life and his family from a distance, they came to the conclusion that he was indeed a great man.

This book is an attempt to remember George the man. I stress the man. George was not flawless. He made mistakes, showed his humanity, and battled with his flesh. George was a man, an imperfect man. Yet there were characteristics within George that I have yet to see manifested in any other individual to the extent that I saw them in George. For this reason, because of the example and the influence of his life, rooted in his desire for Jesus to be his all-in-all, I write this book.

But beyond George the man there exist eternal lessons that all of us need to learn. For those of you who knew George, it is my hope that you will be encouraged and blessed in remembering his life. For those who were not acquainted with George, I pray that this book will be a challenge to you to live a godly life and to strive to make your faith real, vivid, something worth remembering. Finally, I pray that all of our eyes will be further opened to see the harvest fields, for they are ripe unto harvest. Jesus is coming soon!

Stories, memories, trials, victories, and tears. In recalling the memory of George the man, it is my desire that we will see beyond the man to the God whom he served. May our hearts be ignited with a new passion for God, for His people, and for those who have yet to come to know Him.

JED GOURLEY

Bishkek, Kyrgyzstan

March 26, 2013

"Brethren, join in following my example, and note those who so walk, as you have us for a pattern... The things which you learned and received and heard and saw in me, these do, and the God of peace will be with you."

PHILIPPIANS 3:17; 4:9

PROLOGUE

Bishkek, Kyrgyzstan
February 2, 2007 – 11:00pm

The decision was finally made. Evacuation.

George would be flown back to the States for recovery after his extensive operation. He was growing weaker by the hour. I grabbed the phone and placed the call to the emergency number at the U.S. Embassy. Would anyone answer at 11:00 at night?

"Hello, American Embassy Bishkek. How can I help you?" inquired the Duty Officer.

"I am calling about arranging a medical evacuation for a U.S. citizen, George Markey," I answered. After further explaining his recent surgery and his present condition, I awaited a response from the man on the other end of the line.

"Um, yes, I see...," he replied. "Well, I have a few numbers of evacuation companies that you can try to contact, but, really, we will not be able to provide much assistance beyond this."

I asked more questions. I pleaded. I grabbed at straws: "What about the U.S. Air Force base here? They have flights in and out all the time. Couldn't he just be placed on one of those flights?"

However, it seemed that the more questions I asked, the shorter the man's responses grew. Devastated, I pulled out a piece of paper and scribbled down the numbers of evacuation companies as he dictated them to me.

No tears left to cry. No offers of help. Silence filled the house. My father-in-law lay in a dirty hospital in Central Asia with five kinds of bacteria growing inside of him, veins collapsing. Plastic Coke bottles were being used to catch his draining fluids. Furthermore, he had been taken off of antibiotics without our knowledge to supposedly "give his body a rest."

Where was hope?

"Hope thou in God, for I will yet praise Him." (Psalm 42:5,11)
"Give us help from trouble, for the help of man is useless...but I give myself to prayer." (Psalm 108:12; 109:4b)

"Pray. Hope in me. Let them know," I felt in my spirit. I booted up my computer and opened the web browser to the forum where hundreds of people across the world had registered over the previous few days and were praying over the updates regarding George's condition.

Done. Update written and posted. Emails sent. Now to begin calling these evacuation companies...

Then it happened. About 4:00 in the morning our phone rang. Not too unusual with all of the international calls coming in as a result of George's operation. However, when I picked it up this time, I was surprised.

"Hello, is this Mr. Gourley?" the voice asked.

"Yes, it is," I replied.

The voice continued, "I am calling from the U.S. Consulate. We spoke earlier regarding your father-in-law. It seems that you have been very busy tonight."

"What do you mean?" I asked.

"Well, we have been getting calls all night from people in the States, and it seems that you have friends in high places." I didn't know what to say. The only people I had contacted had been those friends and loved ones who had been praying for George. Little did I know how many of these people had been contacting their State Senators and Representatives, former Army buddies, classmates, etc.

The man on the phone continued, "From now until George is evacuated, we will have someone escorting you through this situation."

I sat stunned, grateful to God for His provision. And yet little did I know that this was only the beginning of George's final departure.

SECTION 1

THE DEVELOPMENT OF THE MAN

CHAPTER ONE

"A BIG, STRAPPING MIDWESTERN FARM BOY"

IT WAS PASTOR CHUCK Smith of Calvary Chapel of Costa Mesa who described George Markey as "a big, strapping Midwestern farm boy," in his book *Harvest*. That part of George never really did change, no matter where in the world he lived.

George Winston Markey was born in Dayton, Ohio, on September 28, 1941. His father, William, was originally from a farm near Ladoga, Indiana, to where the family would return in 1948. Coming from a long line of Markeys, who were among the first settlers in central Indiana, George inherited the simple, honest, and hardworking characteristics often seen among farmers in that area. However, it would take many years and periods of breaking for him to be formed into the person God later would use to begin churches around the world.

Not much is known of George's early life in Dayton, but a few memories have come to the surface. Most of them have to do with his willful stubbornness, vast energy, and lack of respect for authority. Rhonda Clark, George's younger sister, recalls a time when they used to live near Patterson Air Force Base. Little George was out throwing rocks one day at the cars that were driving down the road. "He finally hit one," she says, and the car came to a screeching halt. George was in trouble, but the excuse he gave was that he was "trying to build a pile of rocks on the other side of the road."

"Marion, we'll never raise him," said George's father, William. The energy mixed with stubbornness would be a hindrance in George's life, but would also be a tremendous asset when tempered by God with love and generosity. It was there in Ohio that George's mother had the difficult task of keeping track of young George. At one point she had to get a rope and harness and fasten him to the clothesline so that he would not climb over the fence, possibly getting hit by a car. George would often recount that story to the various congregations he pastored. He became a firm believer in disciplining children because of the lack of discipline in his own life.

Another memory from the Markeys' time in Dayton, Ohio, was when George was only about 5 years old and was sitting in the back seat of the family car. As his father was backing out of the driveway, he asked George whether any cars were coming. George, who never even looked to see whether there were any other cars, replied in the negative. The result was a collision and George's father once again testifying to his wife, "We'll never raise him. He's not going to live long enough to graduate from high school."

LADOGA – THE CALL OF THE FARM

It was on May 9, 1947, that George's grandfather, George William Markey, a "prominent and well-to-do farmer" as the obituary reads, was out plowing the fields on his tractor early in the morning. Suddenly, the distant humming of the engine stopped. As the hired hand came running to check on him, it was discovered that he had fallen off of his tractor and had died beneath the heavy machine. After the funeral, which took place in the downstairs parlor of the farmhouse, his widow, Alverda, pleaded with her son, William, to move back home from Dayton with his family and to take care of the farm. William was working in the post office and "never wanted to be a farmer," George later recalled of his father, but they returned to the farm in central Indiana to help George's grandmother in 1948.

Rhonda, George's sister, tells of life on the farm, growing up as kids. "There was an old coal stove. The hired hand lived out in the woods behind the farmhouse. We drank raw milk. Pigs would run in and out of our kitchen, and we fed the piglets from a bottle." Rhonda's job was to carry the water and feed the cattle, while George did the heavy handling of the hay. George's older sister, Laura, would wash the milk cans, but was of little help because of a debilitating mental condition. Life on the farm was not easy, being especially difficult for George's mother, Marion, who was not happy about the move.

Ladoga, Indiana, is a small town with a population of less than one thousand people. The story is told that it was originally named after the largest lake in Europe, Lake Ládoga, situated near St. Petersburg, Russia. Ladoga was the town nearest to the farm and the place where George would spend his late childhood years, his adolescence, and much of his adult life as well. It is interesting that from this country farm adjacent to a small Midwestern town named after a place in Tsarist Russia, one day a rural American family would venture with the Gospel into the cities of the former Soviet Union. But that part of the story comes later.

Family was important to George. There would be times later in life when he would take his own family to cemeteries in Ladoga and nearby New Ross in order to give them a sense of his history. He kept newspaper clippings of some events, including his grandfather's obituary. However, as with many of us growing up, family gatherings are not always considered a priority when we are children, but only later do we see the importance of these relationships.

George understood that these were some of the deepest ties that bind people to one another, and his desire was to see these ties used for the kingdom of God. His mother's family, the Hanners, were from Rockville, Indiana. Later in life George would visit them as a believer, even on his sporadic return visits from the mission field. His desire was that his relatives would see the change in him that God had wrought, and through his example be brought into a saving relationship with Jesus.

In the various churches in which he served, George would often inquire about congregants' family members by name, problems, and struggles that they were going through. Like his dad, George could recall names, birthdays, and telephone numbers with amazing precision. In fact, his dad, William, had memorized the birthdays of all of his relatives down to third and fourth cousins. This trait not only allowed George to connect with people, but, more important, enabled him to show his true concern for them and their families. On more than one occasion, a birthday or anniversary card arriving in the mail with a personal message written inside would show many people George's true interest in them as a person.

CHAPTER TWO

LET THE GOOD
TIMES ROLL

GEORGE HAD ALWAYS been known for wanting to have a good time. "Fun" is a word that many people use when describing him. Classmate Frank Cating recalls one of the times when he visited the Markey home for supper. "George's mother fixed supper and we all sat down to the table. I took a drink from my glass and milk ran all down my chin and neck. I wiped it off and tried again and the same thing happened. The whole family started laughing, and only then did I notice the tiny hole in the middle of the flower on the glass."

George played tricks not only on his friends, but also on his teachers in school. Rhonda, his sister, reminisces about a time when George had to do a book report, and if the book was not on the approved list it had to be personally agreed on by the teacher. "Well, George brought in a book called The First Four Years or something like that. 'Miss Marshall, what do you think about this book?' George inquired. 'Well, it looks a little thin, George,' she said. George told her that perhaps it was because the print was so small and that she should take a look. She opened it, got an electrical shock, and threw the book up into the air."

But at times George could go too far with his practical jokes. Frank Cating recalls the time when the school had just paid to have all of the desks sanded and varnished. Frank shares, "We had this one teacher, 'Doc' Neff, and when we went into his class he said, 'I don't want anybody to write anything on the desks.' Well, guess what? George did! Doc Neff really worked George over, something teachers wouldn't get away with today, but something that was probably very needed for George. And after that, George still had to sand the desk off and redo it."

Another time when George took things too far resulted in his being brought before a local judge. George and a friend had decided to sneak into a nearby school, take all of the books out of every locker, and put them in a huge pile in the middle of the school. When caught, they were brought before the local judge. George was told by Judge Sommer, "Nothing good is ever going to come from your life."

FAST AND FURIOUS

Growing up in the country gives one the opportunity to sometimes drive a little faster than one should. It is tempting to ignore the speed limit signs on the long, straight country roads. In fact, George grew up with the desire to someday be a race-car driver. For the many people who would drive with him throughout his life, perhaps this helps us understand more of why George drove the way he did, although it doesn't excuse it.

In high school, George took a Model-A two-seater and cut the top off with a blowtorch in order to make it into a convertible. He and his friends would race through the corn fields at breakneck speeds, wind blowing through their hair. Also, every year George would go to the Indy 500 and watch the cars, even going the night before just to make sure that he got a good seat. Later in life George would speak of those races at the Indy 500. I remember sermons in which he would talk about the "Novi" cars. He would say that they were the loudest cars ever to race at Indy. People would come to the race just to watch and hear the sound of their engines, the hair on the back of their neck standing up as the Novi roared past. With a sound similar to that of a fighter plane, it could be heard above all of the other cars when going through the backstretch. The Novi not only was the loudest car on the track but also was faster than the other cars, sporting a new engine design that would not be incorporated into passenger cars until some 50 years later.

George often spoke of how these cars could be compared to many Christians. They start out with a bang and appear to be roaring around the track of

24

life, putting others to shame with their zeal and giftedness. Yet the Novi never won a race, and usually did not even finish the course, just as many believers who begin well may come to the end of their lives not having finished the race. Perseverance! Run to win! Finish well! These would become important themes in George's life. In fact, one of his favorite senior pastor conferences that he attended in southern California was on the topic of "finishing well." As we who are running this race are admonished, "For you have need of endurance, so that after you have done the will of God, you may receive the promise" (Hebrews 10:36).

CHAPTER THREE

WHO AM I? WHY AM I HERE? WHERE AM I GOING?

GEORGE WAS RAISED attending churches, in both Ohio and Indiana. George's mother, Marion, would often play the piano in churches in Ohio. However, when they moved to Indiana she did not play. "The churches there were much more strict," says George's sister Rhonda, "In fact, in one of the churches the men sat on one side of the sanctuary, women sat on the other side, and young married couples sat in the middle."

George grew up with an innate love of music, his parents paying for piano lessons from a young age. However, Rhonda recalls that after two lessons George immediately announced, "This is boring," and then proceeded to turn up the volume on the radio and play by ear. His talent for music led him to being able to play many different instruments, participating in and sometimes directing the school band, as well as leading worship in churches even before he was a Christian. Rhonda remembers that when George would play in church "he would really jazz up the worship." George also took dance lessons, being described as "light on his feet" and "a real lady's man." He was known to be the life of the party.

After graduating from high school, George got a job working at the local book publishing factory, R.R. Donnelly & Sons in neighboring Crawfordsville. Often, after his shift was over, George and the guys would go buy a case of beer and find a spot to sit, drink, talk, and laugh until the sun came up.

When coming home late, he would climb up the front porch columns of the house in order to get into his room unseen. But the feelings of dissatisfaction continued to grow in his heart. Where was he heading in life? What was the purpose of life, the reason for his existence? Later, George would look back on this time and see the emptiness that could not be filled, no matter how much fun or how many friends he had. It was during this time of his life that a co-worker at the factory asked him the simple yet life-altering question, "Have you ever tried Jesus?"

The thought lingered in his mind. "Jesus. Could it be?" The life questions gnawed at him: "Who am I?, Why am I here? Where am I going? Jesus? But there are so many hypocrites. So many who claim to be Christians and yet live their lives in contradiction to their own stated beliefs." He remembered a time in high school when 18 young people supposedly repented and got baptized. "I knew them all. I ran with them all, and I knew that they were no different than before they repented and were baptized." George never played the game, never acted the part just so he could assume the name of "Christian." No, "If I ever do become a Christian, it is going to be the real deal," he said. "I am not going to fake anything. It's going to be all or nothing." He was not going to be lukewarm. George later taught that lukewarm Christians actually create unbelief in the hearts of people. They muddy the waters and leave people in confusion. All or nothing!

It was during this time of questioning and emptiness that God finally brought George to the end of himself. On Easter morning, April 22, 1962, at the age of 21, George Winston Markey walked into a small country church and surrendered his life to Jesus Christ. Love flooded his heart. Love for his family, his friends. A desire to grow in the things of God. George often spoke of the dislike that he had for his father before he became a Christian, and now, awakened in his heart was a love for the very one he had disdained and disrespected. George had always appreciated his mother, but now he saw how he had disregarded her and taken advantage of her as well.

With Jesus as the center of his life, his relationships with people began to change, first and foremost with his parents and siblings. However, from the day that George gave his life to Jesus, less than two months would pass before his mother would be taken from this world. Unexpected. The person he had disregarded for most of his life, whom he was just beginning to love, was gone. Remorse. At the young age of 56, George's mother, Marion Mae Markey, was laid to rest in a small cemetery in the nearby town of New Ross. Regret.

The Sunday after his mother's burial, George made a decision that would become a hallmark of his life. He went to church. Although he had been going to church in the weeks preceding his mother's death, this Sunday seemed different. Not to George, but to everyone else around him. People in church asked, "What are you doing here so soon after your mother's passing? Shouldn't you be home mourning?" George's reply: "Well, where else would I be? This is my family." From this moment on, it became natural for George, even in times of sorrow, tragedy, conflict, misunderstanding, and frustration, to come before the presence of God in the family of God. He understood that this was the only place where true love and real comfort could be found.

True to his proclamation of "all or nothing," George's relationship with God became the center of his life. He did not quit his job and join a monastery, but his life became all about Jesus. George became a true worshiper, presenting his body a living sacrifice, holy, acceptable to God, which was his only reasonable response in view of all that God had done for him (Rom. 12:1-2). Having received the forgiveness, the cleansing, the new life, George was going to live a life renewed and transformed – the dynamic life!

Worship took on a new meaning for George. He later wrote in one of his newsletters, "A Pentecostal woman named Betty was an early influence on my life. Betty loved to invite anyone from the local country church to gather and sing around her piano. How glorious it was to sing songs such as 'This World Is Not My Home,' 'Won't It Be Wonderful There,' and 'I'll Fly Away.' In fact, most of the songs we sang were about heaven, and they would have an influence on my future lifestyle. Abraham counted himself as a 'stranger' and pilgrim here, looking for a heavenly city. He that has this hope in him purifieth himself, even as He is pure (I Jn. 3:3). What is the result of this hope? Holy Living. Has the church forgotten its pilgrimage, its destiny? I have always believed that soon, I am going Home to see the King – My Lord and Savior! Hallelujah!"

CHAPTER FOUR

AWAKENING TO GRACE

No one wants to experience loss. The death of a loved one is likely one of the deepest emotional pains that we as humans can feel. The death of George's mother would be the first of many losses, testings, and trials in his life. Coming on the heels of his recent commitment to Jesus was this apparent stripping away of any other preeminent love or foundation other than Jesus. God was at work, fashioning George, continuing to draw him closer and closer to Himself. It was during this time that George would experience an awakening in his life that would propel him forward in his Christian walk.

This awakening came through a man. His name was Lester Swoverland, a member of the church which George had been attending. Les was a dairy farmer by trade, but known to George as a man of the Word, a man of grace. A big, bald man with a huge laugh and a smile from ear to ear, Les, as George often said, could have been a twin to Pastor Chuck Smith. And not merely his appearance, but his love for the Word of God and for people also reflected George's later mentor. Les was known in the community for his generosity. George said, "He would go to the meat market and buy ten packages of meat, which he would then give away to people in need. He would visit people in the hospital, go to people's homes to show his love and support, always thinking of ways to show kindness." Years later, Pam Markey, George's wife, would meet Les and describe him as "an embarrassingly generous man who would never come into the house without giving you something."

In the months following the death of his mother, George spent countless hours with Les in the barn, in his home, on the road, whenever and wherever he could. He was being discipled in the Word, being shown an example of grace, and learning how to love people. However, one evening in particular stood out to George. Their usual time in the barn was filled with biblical inquiries from George and the usual exhortation from Les, "Well, what does the Bible say?" The gentle music in the background continued to play. Les liked to play music for his dairy cows because he said they gave more milk when they were relaxed. When the milking was done, Les invited George to come into the house with him for supper and further conversation.

Betty, Les's wife, greeted George and Les at the door. "Oh, it's you again," she said bitterly while looking at George. George could never figure out how a man of grace like Les was married to such a bitter woman of the law, the complete opposite of Les. One time George recalled driving in the car with both of them, Les behind the wheel and Betty in the passenger seat chewing out her husband for how he was driving. Les would just put his arm around her and laugh, saying, "Oh, Bess, Bess, Bess." That evening as they sat down to dinner, the biblical inquiries continued. "But, Les," George asked, "what does this mean?" He was seeking to know the Word of God. Digging. Examining. Les replied, "Well, let's get out our Bibles. Are you in Romans? What do you think that says?" Daylight fled away. Supper ended, but the conversation continued and it was then that the Word pierced his heart.

George later recalled, "I will never forget that night. For it was then that I saw how wretched of a man I was. My depravity became clear and I saw the grace of God." George drove home that night, eyes filled with tears, mouth filled with praise. "All I could say was, 'Praise God, praise God!'" Out there in the country, it was a rare event when a car would come down the road. "It was the kind of place where when a car drove by everyone in the house got up and looked out the window," George said. "Maybe it was the postman." That night he pulled up to the house and parked the car outside. "George, is that you? Are you coming in?" his father yelled out the door. George answered, "I'll be in in a minute, Dad." He could not bring himself to go inside the house. Tears were streaming down his face, and his father was an unbeliever and would not understand what he had just experienced. George, heart on fire, filled with the Spirit, walked up and down the country road in front of his house, shouting, "Praise the Lord, praise the Lord!" George had been awakened to the grace of God.

Mephibosheth. That is how George saw himself. Few examples of grace are as vivid in the Old Testament as the one found in II Samuel chapter 9. Mephibosheth, the son of Jonathan, was one of the few remaining descendents of King Saul when David began his reign in Israel. Now, normally in those days, when a new king would come to power, immediately he would have executed any remaining relatives of the previous king. "But no," George shared in a teaching. "David sees that it was God who had granted him victory. It was God who had elevated David to the place of honor. For Israel, great victories had been won and the nation was prospering." David had been the recipient of the grace of God, and now he wanted to bless others. "David was thinking back," George continued. "He remembered the covenant he had made with Jonathan. For he said, 'Is there not still someone of the house of Saul to whom I may show the kindness of God?'" Grace is not grace unless it is given. A person is not gracious or kind unless there is a beneficiary upon whom that person is lavishing graciousness or kindness.

Mephibosheth was found. He was living in a place called Lo Debar, a name which means "barrenness, no pasture." It was a place of no significance. Further describing himself, Mephibosheth said in so many words that he was as a nobody – "a dead dog." Crippled in both of his feet, he was unable to do anything on his own. From the lineage of Saul, he was undeserving of any kindness. He was a nobody, from no significant place, only deserving of death. Yet David invited him into his presence. Furthermore, David said that Mephibosheth was to sit at his table, the king's table, continually. And on top of all that, David restored to him all the lands of Saul. Was it because of something good or honorable found in Mephibosheth? No, it was because of a covenant of love made decades earlier.

"We are like Mephibosheth," George said in one of his sermons while shuffling dramatically across the floor. "Living without the promise of God, unable to help ourselves. No way to make it. We are beggars pleading for help. And the King says, 'Come!'" Truly, we are spiritual beggars who are not even able to beg. Destitute, wandering in a barren, evil, wicked world. Entrapped by our own sin, selfishness, fleshly cravings. Spiritually as useful as a dead dog, and yet God has shown us grace. For no reason in us, but based on a covenant of love made thousands of years before and planned before the foundations of the world, God invites us to come. In the same message George would define grace as "showing people kindness in spite of who they are." "It's true, it happens." With finger pointing in the air, George exclaimed in one of his messages, "I know what it is to receive God's grace. He has said, 'Come.' The King says, 'Eat at my table forever!'"

CHAPTER FIVE

DEVELOPMENT THROUGH DIFFERENCE

THOSE MONTHS of discipleship with Les would have a greater influence on George's life and future ministry than almost any other time in his life. Besides receiving a firm grasp of biblical doctrine, it was through Les that George was introduced to the writings of great men of the faith such as M. R. DeHaan, Theodore Epp, Donald Grey Barnhouse, and G. Campbell Morgan. In fact, it was Les who gave George most of his first study books, another attribute that George later would seek to emulate in his personal discipleship of other men. Through Les, George also learned about God's purpose and plan for the nation of Israel as being distinct from the Church. He began to develop his understanding of the end times, an eternal hope that would grow to become a solid anchor in the storms of life.

Along with George's increasing spiritual growth came the birth of a desire to teach. George had not yet attended university, having only worked in the factory for those couple of years after high school. The desire to attend university was there, but in the past he had always looked forward to "just going someplace fun." However, now that Jesus had become the center of his life, George began to look for an educational institution where he could continue to grow in his understanding of spiritual things. The Christian Church he was attending was affiliated with a network of colleges located in various parts of the country. George learned of nearby Kentucky Christian College (KCC) in Grayson, Kentucky, and began preparations for attending

KCC in the fall of 1963. However, George would see that getting there was not as easy as it seemed.

William, George's father, had attended university. In fact, it was at Earlham College in eastern Indiana that he and Marion had met. It was William's desire that his children would receive an education. George's younger sister, Rhonda, was already attending university and was being financially supported by their father. However, when George expressed his desire to go to KCC, his father said that he "would not give one cent to that place." Rather than arguing with his father, George began to seek the Lord. He began to pray. Since his father would not support his decision to go to KCC, George could only rely on the Lord. "I sold my car and record player," George said, just so he could get money to make part of the initial payments. Before heading off for Kentucky, George was also surprisingly blessed by a financial gift from his church. These steps of faith, relying on the Lord to provide and not depending on man, would become vital signposts along the road of George's life.

TIME IN THE "PROMISED LAND"

The wooded back hills of eastern Kentucky would become "home" for George for the next four years, and a place that he would later refer to with admiration as the "promised land." In the initial days of meeting with the other students, George recalled, "All of the freshmen guys met together and were sharing what they were going to do after college. Everyone was saying that they were going to become preachers. I said, 'I am not going to be a preacher. Maybe I will teach Sunday School or be an elder some day.'" Little did George know that within a couple of months he would find himself doing that which he had never before envisioned himself doing.

Students from this small-town college often filled in for preachers from nearby country churches. "As one of the student-preachers was returning to the college from preaching, he had car trouble near another church," George shared. "A farmer saw him and came over and inquired, 'Do you know anyone who would teach at this church? Otherwise it will have to close its doors.'" Upon returning to the college, the student-preacher told George the words of the farmer and said that the church was going to close unless George went to preach. "I was asked to go and preach, and I accepted," George recalled. "This was how God placed me in the ministry. It was not of my own doing."

Without a vehicle, George continued to trust in the Lord to provide for his needs. If God wanted him in the ministry, God would provide for his needs. One day George happened to find a bicycle, which became his main method of transportation for the time being. "I would put the bicycle in the back of a friend's car and he would drop me off on his way to preach at another church," George said. After preaching in the church, George would ride his bicycle to visit people in their homes. George continued, "These were the hills of Kentucky. Some of these people had never been visited by a preacher before. No car would go to these places. They were way back in the boonies." In these trips, George saw poverty like he had never seen before. Dilapidated homes, kids without shoes. Family problems, strife, alcoholism. Desperate people in desperate situations. Week after week George continued to serve, and as he continued to faithfully serve, he was often asked to come and lead in song or fill in for pastors at other churches.

George continued to grow in his love and appreciation of music. He saw music as a tool, not only for worship, but also for encouragement and evangelism. While at KCC, George would often lead in singing during the chapel services. He also was influential in bringing a popular gospel quartet to the campus for a "gospel sing." In his later teachings on worship, George would often cite Colossians 3:16, "Let the word of Christ dwell in you richly in all wisdom, teaching and admonishing one another in psalms and hymns and spiritual songs, singing with grace in your hearts to the Lord."

In speaking of George during his university days, fellow student Lynn White says, "George had an overflowing joy of his salvation. There was a glow about him. Like in Nehemiah, 'The joy of the Lord is your strength.' George worshiped God 24/7." Lynn continues, "George had a confidence in his salvation based solely upon what God had done for him." However, that certainty of his salvation, rooted in a strong understanding of the grace of God, would prove to be a point of controversy with many professors and board members at the university.

From his early days at KCC, George saw that his personal understanding of biblical doctrine differed from that of many of his professors and fellow students. Disputes in classes with professors, misunderstandings with classmates who just couldn't understand why he had to be different from everybody else. Tow the line. Don't rock the boat. These were the opinions of the majority. To be saved by grace was one thing, but to live by grace—it seemed as if that way of thinking could not be tolerated. It seemed that people needed to have a fear of losing their salvation. What else would motivate them to holy living? For George the answer was found in the overwhelming and abounding lovingkindness of God—a grace so freely given to a "wretch like me." George would frequently teach that it is actually the grace of God that inspires us and teaches us to live holy lives. As the apostle Paul wrote in his letter to Titus, "For the grace of God that brings salvation has appeared to all men, teaching us that, denying ungodliness and worldly lusts, we should live soberly, righteously, and godly in the present age." (Titus 2:11-12)

"George, we must have a statement of belief from you because we are not going to graduate you without one," ordered Dr. Lusby, then president of the university. It seems there had been an argument among the members of the board of trustees about whether to graduate George because of his differing views on certain doctrines. In speaking of this confrontation George said, "The president then called me a name of another denomination. I said, 'Oh, Mr. Lusby, I am not a _____. I am just a Christian!'" George never did write a statement of belief, but finally, three days before graduation, George was told that it had been decided that he would be permitted to graduate. George would see throughout his life that there would be many other times when he would both grow and be directed by God specifically through seasons of conflict.

CHAPTER SIX

AN INTRODUCTION TO
MISSIONS (HELLO, WORLD)

DURING HIS FIRST YEAR of college, George met yet another man who would become very instrumental in his life. It was a cold February in Kentucky when John Pemberton came to speak at KCC for the mission rally. "Normally, chapel speakers were boring," George remarked. "They would read a passage from the Bible, close it, and speak about something completely different. But this man was different; he spoke with authority," George said regarding Mr. Pemberton. "And he challenged us in missions." It was in hearing of the work of God in Southern Rhodesia, Africa, that George received what he called a "missions heart." And from this time forward, George found ways to support missionaries and the work of God taking place around the world. Later in life when George became a pastor, he even refused to take a full salary from the church, continuing to work as a carpenter, so that the church would be able to give more to missions.

John Pemberton grew up in a Christian home in Gary, Indiana, during the era of the Great Depression. In the years before the entry of the U.S. into the war in Europe, John and his childhood sweetheart, Marjorie, had dreamed of going into the ministry together. However, immediately upon finishing his senior year of high school, John enlisted into military service. Knowing that he would soon be leaving the country, John and Marjorie were married, and John sailed off to war. During his absence, Marjorie continued to live with her mother, awaiting the return of her husband.

While serving with Army Intelligence in Europe, John was taken captive by the Germans during the Battle of the Bulge. Forced to march through the snow with frozen feet, John was packed into a train car with other soldiers who were then sent to the German prison camp Stalag IV-B. After his release, secured by drunk Russians on horseback, John, severely underweight, began the long journey back to his wife, Marjorie. So as not to startle his new bride, he attempted to gain weight while waiting for his ship back to the States. Returning to the States, John now seemed more inclined to pursue a career in business rather than his earlier desire of entering the ministry.

However, the day came when John was asked to share in his home church about his time of liberation from the prison camp. "John came back from the war a chain smoker," Marjorie remembers. "But the night before he was to share in church, John went out all night and prayed. He had some sorting out to do. And he made his promise to the Lord there, saying, 'If I am going into the ministry, it is going to be all the way.'" Freed from smoking and with a renewed passion to serve the Lord, John preached his message that Sunday morning about being liberated from the prisoner of war camp, but more importantly, about the true liberation found only in Jesus Christ. John and Marjorie then began making plans toward the ministry, which first included getting an education at KCC.

During their time in college, John and Marjorie also ministered in country churches surrounding the college. "John did the preaching and I did the singing," shares Marjorie. "We planned to be evangelists and share in revival services; never once did we talk about doing mission work." However, one day "out of the blue" John suggested joining up with a close friend in his radical plan to go to Africa. "Immediately there was an excitement, a feeling that they could win the whole continent of Africa to Christ," Marjorie says. Coming home, John approached Marjorie, saying, "Let's go for a walk near the garden." Marjorie recounts, "John asked me, 'How would you like to go to Africa?'" Seeing Marjorie speechless in the face of his proposal, John quickly and wisely added, "Of course, we could never do anything like that unless we were one." After that conversation John chose not to mention Africa to her again, but prayed and trusted in the Lord to change her heart if this was truly a calling from God.

"PLEASE DON'T SEND ME TO AFRICA"

Marjorie was relieved, thinking that this was the end of her husband's wild idea, and tried to put the thoughts of Africa out of her mind. But they would not leave. "I was disturbed and angry with God," Marjorie says. "I didn't want it to keep coming up in my mind. But it did, and I kept yelling back in my soul to the Lord, 'What about my children? What about my parents? How could I manage? I am not good with languages.' And the more excuses I made, the weaker my excuse became." Finally, Marjorie shares that God grabbed her heart one night with a vivid dream. "I had a dream that I was back on my father's farm in Soddy-Daisy, Tennessee. The tassels of the corn were brown and ready to be picked. I looked and saw the brown tassels, and there in the ears of corn were brown little faces. The dream was so definite that it made me wake up."

Almost a year after John's initial proposal of going to Africa, Marjorie came to John of her own will, sharing with him that the Lord had also been speaking to her about Africa. "The Lord spoke to me, saying, 'I asked your husband to go to Africa. Now it is time for you,'" she recalls. "And then peace and excitement came pouring into my soul. If the Lord promised to take care of the lilies, how much more me. There was still the fear factor, but there was the promise, 'Lo, I will be with you always.' We lived by that, and that has been passed on to our children."

In 1956, the same year that Jim Elliot and four other missionaries were killed by natives in Ecuador, John and Marjorie Pemberton and their three young children, Sherman, Pamela, and John Mark, boarded a ship bound for Africa. Nearly a month passed before they landed on the shores of South Africa, from where they then made the journey to neighboring Southern Rhodesia (modern Zimbabwe).

Life in Southern Rhodesia was much different from life in America. It began as a pioneering work in the bush where necessities such as flour and fuel could be purchased only through long, rough off-road trips into neighboring cities over 100 miles away. There were no bridges and the means to ford rivers had to be discovered. "We lived in a grass hut with a manure floor," shares Marjorie. "I had to learn how to cook in the ground. We also made our own bricks, and John used encyclopedias to learn how to build the mission."

41

Having been granted 100 acres of land by the government with the stipulation that they build a school and two homes for teachers within the first year, the Pembertons "took a step to make the next step." "'I am just one person,' we so often say. 'What can I do?'" states Marjorie. "But God builds on our lives what He wants done. As John, my husband, used to teach, 'We need to make a decision to make a decision.'" Step by step, decision after decision, John and Marjorie would live and serve in Africa for 40 years, some of their descendants continuing to serve there to this day.

As George continued listening to John Pemberton speak of his life and the work in Southern Rhodesia, he was challenged with this knowledge of the spiritual needs of those on the other side of the world. Who would go? Who would tell them? However, besides a burden for missions, George would soon gain something else from the lives of John and Marjorie Pemberton—something that would change his own life.

CHAPTER SEVEN

THE GIRL
FROM AFRICA

IT WAS DURING George's third year of university that he met her. Returning from Africa, Pamela Pemberton, the only daughter of John and Marjorie Pemberton, began attending the same college her parents had attended. Tall, with long, flowing hair, and a smile that immediately captured one's attention, Pamela descended onto the campus and George took notice. She certainly did stand out in a crowd, inheriting not only her physical height from her parents, but also her passion, intellect, and witty sense of humor. But it was not only the physical appearance and social charm that attracted George, he was also growing in his admiration of Pamela's family—their deep respect for one another, values, zeal, and heart for the world. Pam's elder brother, Sherman, had already begun attending KCC the year after George, and the two of them spent many hours together. Marjorie recalls first meeting George when back on furlough: "George treated us like he had never seen a family that was close like this and centered on Christ."

Although Pam's desire was to get into medical school, with the goal of becoming a medical missionary, her parents decided that she needed to spend at least her first two years of college at KCC. In Southern Rhodesia, Pam had spent a lot of her time assisting in operations at the mission hospital in Mashoko. "She would come home smelling of ether," Marjorie tells with a chuckle. "And she would say things to me like, 'Mom, I saw the most wonderful thing tonight. Dr. Pruett had to open the chest and massage the heart to bring this person back to life. Oh, it was wonderful.'" But now finding herself in the States and attending a Bible college, Pam began to focus on getting through these initial two years and then going on to medical school.

GRASPING GOD'S GRACE

In spite of growing up on the mission field, spiritually Pam was not satisfied with her life. "Because of where I was in my Christian walk at that point, in many ways I felt that it was hopeless for me to live the Christian life." Pam continues, "It's not like I was taught that I couldn't know that I was saved, because my dad taught me otherwise. But the question for me was, How can I know I am saved when I have to live up to a certain standard, and I know that I am not doing it? Jesus saved me by His grace, but I felt like I was kept by what I did." Pam would go to bed every night with doubts and frustrations because she had messed up that day in some way. Pam discloses, "Every night I would say in my prayers, 'God, tomorrow I am really going to do it. Please be patient with me. Tomorrow I am going to live the life I am supposed to live.' And it was failure upon failure because I knew I wasn't doing that, and that I couldn't do that." Unable to find the balance, Pam found herself beginning to minimize sin—the next logical step. Pam concludes, "You begin to say that what you are doing isn't really sin and that you're fine, until you actually read the Bible and see that it really is sin." George had been through similar issues in his own spiritual journey and now became the catalyst that the Lord would use in Pam's life to challenge her in her walk and understanding of the grace of God.

George and Pam first met in the dish room at the college, both employed through "work study" programs in order to help pay for college. Most of their initial times together were actually in visits to churches or revival meetings. Sharing about these initial times, Pam says, "One day we were sitting in Sunday school together and I looked over at his Bible. We were studying the Old Testament and there were all these markings in his Bible. I thought to myself, 'What in the world would anyone have to write so much about in the Old Testament?'" Pam shares that, because of growing up in church, she probably knew the stories of the Old Testament better than George. However, George had a way of connecting the Old and New Testaments that she found fascinating.

As time went on, Pam grew in her admiration of George. She began to look for ways just to be with him. With a spark in her eye, Pam remembers, "George would frequently study down in the basement of the biology lab. It was close to the chapel, and I would go play the piano because I knew George was nearby. I just wanted to see him. And since he was studying the Bible I thought, 'Yeah, I can do that.'" Thus began a season of spiritual growth in Pam's life. "George knew where I was in life because of where he had been," Pam shares. "So we began reading Romans together. And he didn't tell me what it said; he would just have me read it. And I was clueless about where he was heading." For Pam the light gradually came on. Finally, one day as she was meditating on these truths, it became clear. "It's nothing I do," Pam declared. "Everything is Him! I don't keep myself; He keeps me!" That understanding of the grace of God would draw her into a closeness and dependency on the Lord that would empower her throughout her life.

SOMETHING SERIOUS

"George this and George that. All full of George," was Marjorie's description of her daughter's letters to the family back home in Africa. "At that point we began feeling that things were getting serious." Soon after this, when back in the States for deputation, John invited Pam and George out to dinner. After the pleasantries and initial conversation were finished, John looked at George and inquired, "So, just what are your intentions toward my daughter?" "George about swallowed his tongue and Pam wanted to crawl under the table," Marjorie recalls John telling her. However, after that first meeting, John Pemberton returned to Africa satisfied with the man who had become the dominant theme of his daughter's letters.

However, not all was smooth sailing for George and Pam. With a seven-year difference between them in terms of age, a two-year difference in terms of college, and an uncertain future in terms of Pam and her medical studies and life pursuits, George did what he felt he must do. He broke off his relationship with Pam. Soon after this devastating decision, Pam returned to Africa on a break from her studies. Sitting in front of the large fireplace in their African homestead in Hippo Valley, weeping and disappointed, Pam recounted the story to her mother. George had told her that she was only 18 and that now was her chance to pursue her desire of being a medical doctor. However, Pam felt that George was just giving her excuses. "She was so angry that she wouldn't even talk with George," Marjorie remembers. "I told her, 'Pam, those are not excuses. That is wisdom. Did you not want to be a doctor? You can't study if you are tied up with raising children. Don't be angry; that is only wisdom.'"

Keeping George at arm's length, Pam returned to college. At the end of her two years at KCC, Pam went on to Indiana University for pre-med studies. George, having graduated from KCC, would drive over to see her at the university from time to time. "She would tell him to get lost, and then he would come back another time only to be sent away again," recalls Marjorie. Pam finished her studies and applied for medical school. However, in those days only three percent of female applicants were accepted into medical school. Pam's letter of rejection soon came in the mail. Devastated, Pam sought solace from her parents while they were visiting in Indiana on furlough.

Continuing to work as a medical technologist in order to pay for her studies, Pam was encouraged and determined to keep trying to enter medical school. "After our furlough we went back to Africa with the feeling of 'What's going to happen now?'" Marjorie remembers. "And we had no sooner arrived in Africa than we received the distorted, long-distance call from Pam. 'Dad, I'm getting maaaarrrried,' Pam said. 'To whom?' John asked. 'Geeeooorge,' Pam answered." With plans for a wedding now being made, John and Marjorie soon found themselves returning to the U.S. John officiated George and Pam's wedding, which was held at Olive Hill Christian church near Grayson, Kentucky, in December 1971.

SECTION 1 PHOTOS

Young George in front of their home in Dayton, Ohio.

George pulling his younger sister Rhonda.

He was an all-American boy, 1952.

Growing up on the farm with his rooster Danny, 1952.

Driving in the "Iron Nash," 1952

George at age 12 sitting on the John Deere tractor, 1953.

George Markey
Agricultural Course
Class Officer 3, 4
Class Play 3, 4
Band 1, 2, 3, 4
Boy's State 3
4-H 1, 2, 3, 4, Officer
3, 4; F. F. A. 1, 2, 3, 4
Officer 3, 4
Yell Leader 3, 4
Business Manager
on Annual Staff
Dance Band 2, 3
Track 1

In High school George was involved in many extra-curricular activities.

George's send-off to KCC by New Ross Christian Church. His father on his right.

The Pembertons in Southern Rhodesia in 1963—Pam is 15 years old.
Back row: Sherman, Pam, John Mark. Front Row: John, Robert, Marjorie.

George and Pam's wedding: George's sister Rhonda, on left.
George's best man on right, December 1971.

SECTION 2

THE DEEPENING OF THE MAN

CHAPTER EIGHT

FOLLOWING
THE SPIRIT

LESS THAN A YEAR before George and Pam were married, George had begun a Christian coffeehouse as an outreach to the youth in the small town of Maysville, Kentucky. In fact, it was while George was driving Pam to Maysville to show her what the Lord was doing there that he proposed to her. George's proposal was really more like a list of reasons why they should not get married. Visibly shocked that he was even mentioning marriage at all, Pam went to visit the ladies' room in order to clear her mind. What was happening? Another sporadic visit from George had stirred up all of the old feelings. "I had just thrown away all of his letters, and everything else having to do with George. I wanted to move on in my life," Pam relates. However, "It was one of those things where God takes something completely away from you and then gives it back to you in His way and in His time." She returned to George, who was sitting in her Ford Falcon in the parking lot of the restaurant—and said yes.

After the wedding, George and Pam settled into the beginning of their family life in the town of Tollesboro, not far Maysville—together at last! However, after just two weeks of married life George and Pam took in their first troubled teen to live with them. Ministering to troubled youth in their own home would become normal ministry for them over the next few years.

With a heart for young people, George continued to work in the coffeehouse there in Maysville. Although it was a successful outreach to the youth in the community, not everyone appreciated its existence. Black teenagers were some of those who visited the center, and many people in this rural white community did not like that. In fact, the mayor of Maysville seemed to be leading the charge in the attempts to shut down the center. George wrote a letter to the editor of the local paper rebutting the mayor's reasons and attempts to close the center. Once again, George was learning through opposition, growing through difficulties.

George was looking for something. The churches in which he had been involved were mostly negative when it came to the idea of reaching out to drug addicts and troubled teens. In fact, George resigned from his position as youth pastor in one church over this very issue. Several drug addicts and musicians had believed in Jesus, but were told that they would not be welcome in the church unless they changed their appearance. There had to be something, somewhere—a place in the Body of Christ for people like this.

ASBURY REVIVAL

For George, his time in Kentucky was a time of searching. Exciting things were happening in various parts of the country. A revival at nearby Asbury Seminary in Wilmore, Kentucky, had begun on February 3, 1970. As students gathered for the chapel service, the Dean of the college did not feel impressed to share a message, and instead he opened up the service to any students who wanted to give testimonies. Students began sharing, confessing sin, coming forward for prayer. The service kept going. The students did not show up for lunch, and classes were canceled for a week. The chapel was full day and night with people seeking God. Hundreds of people from all over the country poured onto campus as news reports circulated about what was happening in Wilmore.

The effects from this outpouring of God's Spirit were being seen throughout the Midwest and beyond. It was said that by the summer of that year, 130 colleges had been affected by that revival. Students would call home to their churches sharing about what was happening, and revival would break out in those churches. Other students began traveling around the country, speaking about what God had done there in Asbury. As revival spread among the churches, people were changed, men and women were called into full-time ministry, and hearts were touched with the need to share the Good News of Jesus with all kinds of people, including hippies, drug addicts, and others who were a part of the unwanted and neglected fringes of society. In quoting Robert Coleman, who wrote about revival, George shared, "Give me one divine moment when God acts and I say that moment is far superior to all the human efforts of man throughout the centuries."

THE BAPTISM OF THE HOLY SPIRIT

The revival at Asbury was another one of the important signposts in George's life. Although himself not a part of the initial revival, George witnessed the effects of this outpouring of God. Soon afterward, George began an in-depth study of the Book of Acts, researching the matter of the filling of the Holy Spirit. Was there such a thing? If so, what was it? Some churches taught that this experience was not for today, rather that it ceased with the death of the last New Testament apostle. Others took an opposing view, saying that not only was it for believers today, but it had to be accompanied by the miraculous gift of speaking in tongues. As George studied, he could see that neither view seemed to be supported by a clear reading of the biblical texts. Having read and reread, researched, and critically examined every passage in the Book of Acts that mentioned the baptism or filling of the Spirit, as well as other portions of Scripture, George came away from his study a firm believer in the reality of and need for the filling of the Holy Spirit. George and Pam felt that there must be a church somewhere that held a balanced biblical view of the Holy Spirit, untouched by either tepid traditionalism or extravagant experientialism.

One of the churches that George had been attending during this time was a small Methodist church in the nearby town of Tollesboro. There was a young minister serving in this church who also had been challenged by what was happening in Wilmore. In fact, similar things began happening in his church as well, to such an extent that the little church was now packed on Sundays with people crowding out the front door. Young people were getting saved. People were being filled with the Spirit, emboldened to share the Gospel. When similar things began occurring at the coffeehouse, George came and spoke with this pastor about what was happening. The pastor's explanation of the gifts of the Spirit was in agreement with the conclusions that George had derived from his own personal studies of Scripture. However, just as these exciting changes began taking place in the church, this young pastor became ill with a virulent strain of leukemia and went home to be with the Lord. Unfortunately, with his passing the openness to the things of the Spirit at this church also passed.

"Oh, how we need Him! How our churches need Him. We must be dependent upon the Holy Spirit!" was a message that George frequently shared. Truly, we must drink of the living water so as to have the strength to live for Jesus, the joy to radiate Jesus, and the peace to rest in Jesus. The filling of the Spirit is, without a doubt, one of the most important themes in the Book of Acts. George taught, "In reality, it should be called the 'Acts of the Holy Spirit' rather than the 'Acts of the Apostles,' for it is the Holy Spirit who is working in and through His chosen vessels." The moment we cease needing the wisdom, power, and inspiration of the Holy Spirit is the moment we begin depending on our own fleshly resources, knowledge, and strength. Thus, the Christian life loses all essence of the supernatural life, and simply becomes an expression of who has the better plan for saving souls, the brighter style of preaching, or the more benevolent humanitarian program. Without a theology of, and dependence on, the Holy Spirit, the Christian life becomes all about our walls, gates, and fortifications, rather than about effecting change, overcoming obstacles, and being a bold and powerful witness to the world.

George continued, "There is a purpose for the power, a reason. I don't care what you call it, the baptism of the Holy Spirit or the filling of the Holy Spirit. I am not going to argue terminology. But the important question today is, do you have this dynamic in your life? For you cannot be an effective witness apart from the power of the Holy Spirit." With that empowering of the Holy Spirit comes a boldness to stand for Jesus, an overwhelming love for His people, and a desire to influence others for the kingdom of God.

THE SEARCH CONTINUES

George's heart was to be used by the Lord to touch as many people as possible. And that desire to influence young people inspired him to work with the Boy Scouts. During the summer of 1972, George was working as aquatics director at Camp Oyo near Portsmouth, Ohio. "It was family night, Thursday night," long-time friend Joe Bruch recalls. Joe's brother, Bill, was attending the camp as a Scout, and Joe came to visit him. Himself a believer in Jesus for less than a year, Joe exuded an excitement about his salvation. George noticed the large wooden cross that Joe wore around his neck and began asking him about it. "I began to tell George that there was a real move of the Lord in Portsmouth, that many young people were coming," recounts Joe. "This got George excited."

George, constantly seeking to be where the Holy Spirit was moving, barraged Joe with questions: What church was he going to? What kind of people were welcome there? Joe told him of a church that had only recently begun, and about Jim Sharp, a member of the church who had been a student at Asbury during the revival there. Jim had returned from Asbury, sharing with what was then a small group of believers, and the Lord began to work in the hearts of the people. "Soon the church was already having two services, and people would run out after the first service and get in line for the second service," Joe shares. "People would even bring their animals to church." Hippies were among those who were getting saved, and cars had to park blocks away from the Seventh-day Adventist church building that this young fellowship was renting. George and Pam drove up to Portsmouth one Sunday, and when they walked in, they could sense the presence of God. That very summer George and Pam decided to move from Maysville, Kentucky, to Portsmouth, Ohio.

The Christian music festival Ichthus was also partially birthed out of the revival that happened in Wilmore. Fresh music is often one of the results of a move of God. As hundreds and thousands of people were being moved by God's Spirit, those natural responses of worship at the seminary in February 1970 turned into a multiday outdoor Christian music festival in the summer of that year. Joe went to Ichthus that year and pitched his tent at a crowded place in front of the college dorms. George, always at ease in talking with people, instead inquired of a local farmer who lived near the festival grounds as to the possibility of using his property to make camp for his large group. Separated from the crowds at the main festival site, the peaceful atmosphere easily facilitated discussions around the campfire. The Word was powerfully shared at these festivals, and it was at one of the first Ichthus music festivals that a pastor shared something that rang true with George and stuck with him for the rest of his life: "The most important thing is to see where the Holy Spirit is moving and get into the flow of the Holy Spirit." The Ichthus music festival, and that peaceful farm in particular, became the place where church groups would venture annually under George's leadership for the next two decades.

CHAPTER NINE

IT BEGAN
IN A STABLE

GEORGE AND PAM'S TIME in Portsmouth was marked by continual outreach and deep fellowship. "George was always taking us kids camping and spelunking," recalls Joe Bruch. "We would hang up a lantern and swim in the cave streams. At night the rats would carry away our stuff deep into the caves." Pam remembers a Bible study that was started in a garage. "It was spontaneous, a real work of the Spirit," she says. Also, every Sunday after church, groups of people would head down to Lake Roosevelt for picnics and fellowship. The lives of George and Pam were open. "There were people coming in and out of their house 24/7," Joe remembers. "They did not even lock the doors."

The Book of Acts was being lived out in Portsmouth: "And they continued steadfastly in the apostles' doctrine and fellowship, in the breaking of bread, and in prayers" (Acts 2:42). For George, the model of the New Testament became crucial to his understanding of the modern, local church and its purpose. A book that had been given to him by a group of believers in Louisville opened his eyes to the importance of the New Testament as our example. The book, The New Testament Order for Church and Missionary, written by long-term missionary Alexander Rattray Hay, examines the energy, effectiveness, and expansion of the first century church. In fact, the first part of this book is basically an exposition of the Book of Acts. However, as is mentioned in the preface to the book, "The New Testament method is as dead as any other method if it is applied without the guidance and power of the Spirit Who alone gives it life" (Hay 1960, 10).

With George's love for music and the Word, his desire to reach out to youth, and his previous experience with the coffeehouse in Maysville, George soon sought to open a coffeehouse in Portsmouth. The pastor of the young fellowship in Portsmouth knew the owners of a local Christian bookstore. The second floor of that building had been used in the past as a stable for horses. Gathering young people from the church, George set about cleaning up the stable and removing the dividers between the stalls, replacing them with tables. They aptly named the coffeehouse "The Stable."

"George brought in bands like Honeytree, Simple Truth, Petra, and Phil Keaggy," recalls Joe. "It was open Friday and Saturday nights, and was so packed that all the kids couldn't even get in. The bands would play and share, there would be testimonies, Bible studies, and skits put on by the kids." Often the bands who were playing at the coffeehouse would spend the night at George's house and continue to fellowship until late at night. The coffeehouse was a great success, and it worked in tandem with the church there in Portsmouth.

George's heart for ministering to youth also led him to take in troubled kids to live with them. While in Maysville they took in their first girl, Debbie. Upon moving to Portsmouth, George continued to look for opportunities to serve young people in this way. Their first home in Portsmouth, on Grant street, was too small for what they had in mind, and George began looking for other opportunities. One day, the City of Portsmouth advertised a sealed-bid sale of the "Fresh Air Camp for Youths." It was a large property with a swimming pool, two dormitories, a big commercial kitchen, and much more. George was immediately interested.

Ernie Kennard was a realtor whom George had met when he first came to Portsmouth. Also a believer, and one with whom much time in fellowship was spent, George approached Ernie for advice about participating in this sealed bid. "The city had not issued a starting bid, and George wanted to know what the property was worth," remembers Ernie. "As a realtor, I advised him that the bids would probably begin at $35,000 and go up.

Since I knew several people who would probably be interested in buying a property like that, I advised George to offer at least $35,000 if he really wanted to acquire the property." George prayed and trusted God with this property and the future ministry that could be done through it. He decided that he would bid $15,000. "Ernie thought he was crazy," remembers Joe Bruch. "There was no way that a bid like that would get this property." Stubbornly refusing Ernie's advice, George prepared to make a bid of $15,000. In a last-ditch effort to help, Ernie gave some final advice. "I encouraged George to add $100 to his bid just in case someone else was thinking like George. Well, George reluctantly agreed and then we prepared the bid and delivered it to the City Manager's Office." One week later, on the day the bids were to be opened, George and Ernie went to the office. At 2:05 pm an attendant invited them into the Manager's Office. Ernie continues, "Seeing no other people present and only one bid on his desk, he opened George's bid, smiled in amazement, and said to George, 'It looks like you have bought the property for $15,100.' At that, George laughed and said, while smiling, 'Thanks, Ernie. You just cost me an extra $100!'" For Ernie, Joe, and others there in Portsmouth, this was a valuable lesson on prayer, listening to God, and waiting for His direction.

A TIME OF INFLUENCE

After purchasing the camp, George began making the necessary repairs, even constructing an additional room for Pam and himself. Soon after the purchase, a local judge telephoned George, asking if he would be interested in taking in some boys who were leaving prison and transitioning back home. George agreed and they began housing these boys, since the girls who were living with them had already left. "George took the boys on all of his carpentry jobs," Pam shares. "While I was teaching at a nearby college, the boys would go with George everywhere he went." George's method of discipleship was not so much in just teaching a Bible study or program, although he did that as well, but in sharing his life, time, and resources in ways that would make a lifetime investment into a person.

George was also the unofficial youth pastor at the church there in Portsmouth. He was never paid, nor did he believe that he should have been paid. In fact, George mortgaged his own property in Ladoga, Indiana, so that the church could build a facility there in Portsmouth.

Ministry for George was a natural overflow of his relationship with Jesus, not something that was done only if he was asked or paid. Ministering to people was his life, and people understood that, valued it, and trusted George.

Concerning how these young people trusted and looked up to George, and how much George would take care of them, Pam recalls the following story. "There was this one guy who was the town bully. He was chasing Chris Neff, one of the young guys in the church. Chris ran to our house and George went out to meet him. The guy who was following Chris had a baseball bat and chased him up onto our porch. George kept telling this bully that he loved him and that Jesus loved him, but George also told him that he needed to back off and not swing that bat." Susie Bruch, Joe's wife, was at George and Pam's house at the time and remembers looking out the front window and seeing an entire gang of thugs brandishing bats and chains as they awaited the orders of their leader. Pam continues, "Well, the guy swung it at George, and George grabbed the bat and used it to take him down. The local judge told George that the guy had needed that for a long time. George went to visit the man in the hospital, but when he was released from the hospital he did not show his face in town for the next six months because he was so ashamed."

Besides making people feel safe and protected, George also made people feel valuable, important. "George would always talk about things with you and say, 'Well, what do you think?'" Joe shares. "I thought to myself, 'I'm nineteen and you're the leader. What do you care what I think?' But he was always interested in even what young people thought. Whether he agreed with you or not, he was interested in what you had to say. And he was sincere when he asked you your opinion." George's influence on the young people at that time is felt and remembered to this day. "He made you feel like you were important," continues Joe. "I always felt that George had more confidence in me than I had in myself."

ALWAYS REACHING OUT

"George had bought this old Ford van from the mortuary," Joe shares. "We young people went with George everywhere in that van to share the Gospel. However, we probably pushed it more than rode in it—it was always breaking down. We would go into bars to evangelize and people would throw beer at our feet. They did not want to hear the Gospel," Joe recalls. "I remember one man that was sitting at a bar wearing army fatigues. George talked to him as he drank and gave him a tract. He put it in his pocket. Two weeks later he put his jacket on, felt the tract, read it, and got saved. He is still walking with the Lord, teaching and serving in church. He even sent support to George and Pam on the mission field, but secretly so that they would not know."

Joe continues, "I worked at the community pool and had the keys to the pool. When people would get saved, I would open up the pool at night and we would go in and have baptisms." George, always seeking to take the Gospel to as many people as possible, even had kids sharing their testimonies and songs on television. Groups of youth were going into the Kiwanis club and sharing with businessmen, lawyers, and doctors about what had happened in their lives. Susie Bruch recalls answering the phone one morning and hearing George telling her of an opportunity to share her testimony at the Kiwanis club later that day. "I wasn't ready and didn't feel that I could share in front of all of those businessmen and doctors, but George wouldn't take no for an answer and so I went."

Susie also remembers one Thanksgiving celebration there in Portsmouth as families and friends from the church were planning to celebrate a big meal together. "It was the first turkey that I had ever cooked. George came in the house and told us about one family who didn't have any food. I told George that I didn't even know how this turkey was going to turn out. Well, George told me not to worry and that it would be great. He kept coming over to check on that turkey, and when it was done we packed it up and took it to that family."

NOTHING SHORT OF A MIRACLE

Before Pam was married, in a visit to the doctor before their wedding, she had learned that she would never be able to have children. However, this news had not really affected her at the time. "I had been very influenced by university teachings about overpopulation," Pam discloses. "I thought that it would be irresponsible to bring children into this world. Instead, I thought that perhaps we should adopt or take in people." However, after Pam and George were married, there came a definite change in her desire to have children.

"I so want to give you a grandchild," Pam now wrote in her letters to her mother. Sadly, after three years of marriage and numerous doctor visits, the conclusion of the medical community remained the same: George and Pam would never be able to have children. At the time, Pam was continuing to teach medical technology at a nearby state college. Pam's mother, Marjorie, recalls the story. "Pam was teaching a class on how to use a specimen to determine pregnancy, and she used her own specimen. The result was positive, and the class gave her a standing ovation." Pam was shocked. A few days later, George came home from a prayer meeting smiling, sharing that they had just prayed that they would have a boy. Pam, in bed with severe morning sickness, was upset at George's news and shared that she had been wanting and praying for a girl. In a remarkable bit of irony, not only was Pam pregnant, but she was pregnant with twins – a boy and a girl.

A TIME OF TENSION AND TRANSITION

Spontaneous times of prayer, deep fellowship, the gifts of the Spirit in operation, people getting saved—all of these things were visible fruits of a glorious work of God that was taking place in Portsmouth. However, there came a time when the Lord would allow disagreement and discouragement to be the method of deepening George's dependence on Himself, as well as directing him into the next plans that He had for him.

A pastor from another church in the area, who also had been involved in the coffeehouse ministry with George, began inviting kids to his house for Bible studies. "He was allowing things to go on that really were upsetting to George," Joe remembers. "Kids were making wine and drinking at his house, and George wanted the leadership of our church to confront this other pastor." George's pleas, however, seemed to fall on deaf ears, and the man was not confronted. At the same time, this spontaneous and spiritual work that the Lord was doing at the church in Portsmouth seemingly began to be controlled by the leadership. Pam shares, "What people were already doing spontaneously and by the direction of the Holy Spirit in the church, the leadership was now trying to control and organize." Due to these and other issues, a rift formed between George and the leadership of the church. When the leader was unwilling to even pray with George over the matter, George threatened to set up a tent in front of the leader's house until he would pray with him. However, seeing that the issues were not being resolved and not wanting to cause further division, George decided to quietly leave the church, not even telling his closest friends there what was happening. It was not his desire to split the church, but rather to maintain the unity of the bond of peace (Eph. 4:3).

Pam awkwardly continued going to some of the meetings without George, saddened over the tension and loss of relationships. Joe and others, confused by George's absence, attempted to get him to come back. But there was no return. "George went into a time of depression," Joe recalls. "He would not even get out of bed. I never thought anything could faze George. He always took the bull by the horns, but when it came to spiritual things his heart was very tender." The time came for the annual trip to Ichthus, and George managed to pull himself out of his bed and head off for the trip. "George went to take the group, but ended up leaving them on the way down and hitchhiking home," Pam remembers. "I was in Grayson visiting family when I heard, and I immediately went back to Portsmouth. George was lying in bed saying that it was 'an effort just to breathe.' I was worried." All throughout Pam's pregnancy, George was in some kind of depression over what had happened there in Portsmouth.

Although George was not attending church at this time, he was in the Word all the time. "He was always reading his Bible, and he read Watchman Nee's books The Normal Christian Life and The Release of the Spirit," recalls Pam. "People would come over to the house to try to 'straighten him out,' telling him that he needed to 'get right with God.' They were Job's comforters." But one man helped George through this time. Pam continues, "Ernie Kennard," the realtor mentioned earlier, "would come over and take George out to breakfast. George would talk, and Ernie would listen." Eventually, what had been a time of mourning over the loss of what could have been, turned into a time of seeking the Lord concerning what He had next for George and Pam.

TEACHING BY THE FIREPLACE

Of course, what was next for George and Pam was the birth of their first children. Continuing to teach at the local college became more and more difficult for Pam as the precious little lives grew inside of her. Having been warned by her doctor that there could be severe problems unless she got off her feet, Pam approached the leadership of the college requesting to be released from her contract. In view of her skills as a teacher and the rapport that she had with the students, the Dean of the college was hesitant to release her and pleaded with Pam to continue teaching the students, even at her home. Marjorie, Pam's mother, remembers, "At the time they were living at a huge, cold place. So Pam would sit in a rocking chair by the fireplace with her feet up, and there were forty students on the floor around her." Pam managed to get all of her students through the exams, and then on the day of their wedding anniversary in December of 1975, Renee and George were born at Scioto hospital in Portsmouth.

CHAPTER TEN

SEEKING
A MODEL

WITHOUT THE SPIRITUAL support of the church, George and Pam felt that they could not continue to house the kids who had come to them from such troubled backgrounds as prison, broken homes, and drug abuse. The varied and difficult situations that would arise in this kind of ministry required the loving care, prayers, and encouragement of the body of Christ. For example, during their time of housing and ministering to girls, Debbie, the first girl they had taken in to live with them, pulled a knife on Pam. In the ensuing struggle it was obvious that the battle for these kids was not against flesh and blood, but rather against the rulers of the darkness of this age (Eph. 6:12). Finally able to free herself, Pam proceeded to lovingly calm down Debbie, who then burst into tears and apologized for what she had done. On another occasion, one of the girls they had taken into their home had gotten pregnant. Without George and Pam's knowledge, she was quietly absconded by an influential "Christian" woman in the community to get an abortion secretly in New York.

As George and Pam began phasing out this ministry, one event in particular clearly confirmed that now was the time to end it. Marjorie, Pam's mother, had come to help with the birth and initial care of the twins. Marjorie loved these kids who had been staying with George and Pam, and she sought to minister to them through her joyful, caring, yet strong demeanor. A powerful woman of the Word and prayer, Marjorie would speak straight to the hearts of the kids. However, one day $100 went missing from Marjorie's wallet. In view of this and other issues, George decided that it was time to move the boys out, especially with the lack of spiritual support from the church as well as the new responsibility of having his own children.

As the last of the boys was moved out, the city of Portsmouth contacted George, desiring to buy the camp back from him. They offered $30,000 for it, twice the amount he paid for it, and gave them 30 days to move out. With no place to go and not knowing what they were going to do, George and Pam continued to seek the Lord. Days and weeks passed without any options, but George and Pam knew that the Lord would provide. Even when doubt crept into their minds and hearts, they continued to wait upon the Lord, trusting in Him. Realtor Ernie Kennard had been frantically searching for a place for George and Pam, and had all but given up hope of finding anything. Pam remembers, "Ernie would call all the time and say, 'I just can't find anything.'" Twenty-four hours before they had to be out of the facility, Ernie heard of an estate sale in the nearby town of Wheelersburg and relayed the news to George. The cost was $10,000 for an acre of land and a small house that needed a lot of work. George jumped at the chance, moving the family into the first floor of this house while repairing the second story. God had provided, and the "unexpected" discovery of this lot was yet another faith-expanding time for Ernie.

GO WEST, YOUNG MAN

George, always good with his hands and physically very strong, got started on repairing the house, ripping off the roof down to the beams. During this time, George began reading a book titled Brethren, Hang Loose, by Robert Girard. The back cover of this book states that the author was writing "out of frustration with the institutional, evangelical church, its inability to give control of itself to the Holy Spirit, its preoccupation with secondary things, and its lack of spontaneity, freshness and genuine spiritual power." Pam remembers, "George was excited about what this guy was saying about what church should be like." The more George read, the more he wanted to see for himself the things that were described in the pages of this book.

The twins were four months old at the time of the move from the large property in Portsmouth to the small house in Wheelersburg, and Pam was just finishing her teaching contract with the university. Within a couple of months, the repairs of the house were completed, and George decided that he wanted to visit the church written about in the book that he had been reading. However, Scottsdale, Arizona, the city where the church was located, was not a short drive away. Discouraged by what they had experienced in Portsmouth yet expectant that the Lord had something else for them, George and Pam began to make plans for an extended trip out West. "We sold our house for a profit, bought a van, and had a huge garage sale," Pam recalled. "Anything else that was left we put in George's sister's garage and went out West."

George lived what he taught. Often, he would teach about not "driving your tent pegs in too deep." For George, a big part of living by faith involved being willing to part with earthly goods, familiar places, and even close friends in order to follow the leading of the Spirit. He did not seek the acceptance of the world or the supposed security it had to offer through the accumulation of things, but rather he recognized that he was a stranger and pilgrim during his journey here on earth (Heb. 11:13). "This world is not my home; I'm just a passing through," George would frequently remind congregations in his sermons. In their pursuit of the Lord and desire to be where the Spirit was moving, George and Pam pulled out their tent pegs, packed up the van, and embarked on a new venture in faith.

After having camped out all the way to Arizona, George and Pam, upon arriving in Scottsdale, splurged and spent the night in a motel. The next morning, full of expectation that they were now going to see that for which they had been longing, George and Pam went to visit the church mentioned in Brethren, Hang Loose. However, they soon discovered that this was not all that they had expected. Regarding that time, Pam shares, "We were a little disappointed with the meeting itself because we did not sense that freedom and joy of which we had read in the book. However, we were sure that when we met the pastor and told him where we were from, that we had read his book, and that we were excited to see this body of believers in action, that at the least he would want to schedule a time to meet with us and discuss in person what the Lord was doing there. When we greeted him after the service, he shook our hands and said something mundane like, 'How nice that you read my book,' and dismissed us. It was a very discouraging moment. I think we had put all our hopes in this church and being able to really stay for a while and observe how things were supposed to be under the control of the Holy Spirit. It was obvious to both of us right away that this wasn't where we were to be. It just wasn't for us." What was next? What should they do now? Where should they go? They could return to Portsmouth, but George felt that doing so would be divisive. Unsure of what to do, they decided to make one more trip.

"CHECK OUT CALVARY CHAPEL"

Back in the Midwest there was a man who had heard of something exciting that was happening in a church in southern California called "Calvary Chapel." He kept telling George that he should check out Calvary Chapel while he was out West. George shared, "So, just to shut this guy up, we decided that we would go visit this place. But in our hearts we did not expect to see much of anything at all." Arriving into southern California in the summer of 1976, George and Pam's search brought them to a church called Calvary Chapel of Costa Mesa, which was pastored by Chuck Smith.

In the late 1960s and early 1970s, there were fresh works of the Spirit springing up in different parts of the Unites States. What had happened in Wilmore, Kentucky, to an even greater extent was happening in southern California. Two people in particular were sensitive to this move of God. Chuck and Kay Smith, also having gone through a season of dissatisfaction with overorganized, denominational churches, were deeply touched with the need to minister to those whom traditional churches had been ignoring. Society was in a general state of rebellion, and the youth of America were experimenting with anything and everything in the name of love and peace. However, as many of them would discover, after the initial sensations of freedom and ecstasy waned, the lingering feelings of hopelessness and enslavement remained. By the thousands, everyone from surfers to hippies began discovering that true peace and love are found only in a dying to self and an embracing of the One who gave Himself to redeem us from our sin. Chuck and Kay Smith began receiving these young people who were often rejected from other churches simply because of their appearance. The term "Jesus People" became a way of describing these young people.

In the summer of 1976, George and Pam walked into the sanctuary of Calvary Chapel of Costa Mesa and, immediately, were amazed at what they witnessed. There were so many people that they had to sit on the floor in between the aisles. Freedom. New songs filled the air. The Word was taught simply, yet powerfully. True Grace. At the end of the service, grandmothers and hippies were standing arm in arm singing to the Lord. There was a sincerity and spiritual reality that could not be explained. An abundance of love and joy. "We couldn't leave," George said. "We were so moved by the Holy Spirit." Their planned "quick visit" would turn into a six-month extended stay.

"We're going to find a house on the beach," George told Pam. Not only Pam, but everyone who heard George's idea thought that he was crazy for even thinking about looking for a house on the beach. It would be too much money. At the time George and Pam were living off the proceeds of the houses that had been sold in Ohio. "I found a house that belonged to a contractor who was going to tear it down in a month," George shared. "We paid $275 per month, and the neighbors said that they normally would charge that amount, or more, for only a couple of days." The contractor ended up not tearing down the house, and for the next six months the Markeys lived there. Little George and Renee, the twins, learned how to walk on Newport Beach.

"In Calvary I learned a pattern for ministry," George recalled. "It would become a model for the rest of my life." With so much happening at this church, George got involved in as much as he could. He volunteered to work in the children's ministry just so that he could see how it worked. He became a part of one of the first "Shepherd's Schools" in order to glean principles of ministry and refine his understanding of scriptural truths. George and Pam were listening to Pastor Chuck's previous messages on tape, as well as making it to every service that they could. Each time, they would sit in a different part of the church in order to talk with as many people as possible. "Everyone had a testimony and the conversations were always about the Lord," recalls Pam.

"We would sometimes visit other churches in the area, but never wanted to miss a service at Calvary," Pam shares. "There was this one time when we were visiting a church, and the first thing the pastor had the people do was to stand up when they had donated a certain amount of money." Upon hearing the words of the pastor, George and Pam looked at each other and whispered, "Let's leave." Somehow managing to extract the kids from the nursery without too many questions, George and Pam were on their way back to Calvary Chapel. Racing back, George got pulled over for speeding in his attempt to make it back for the last service at Calvary. Pam continues, "When we tried to add more to our time in California, it was as if God was saying, 'This is what I have for you right now. Go to Calvary.'"

Sunday after Sunday they heard the announcement—a trip to Israel. Although George never mentioned it, Pam knew that he really wanted to go. "I just could not imagine getting around southern California and taking care of the twins without him, so I resisted it," Pam remembers. Finally, one Sunday evening Pastor Chuck announced that places for the Israel trip were filling up rapidly, and that if anyone was interested in going they should sign up in the office. "I leaned over and told George that I thought that he should go and sign up," continues Pam. "George was surprised. He had never left the country. He did not even have a passport." As Pam released George to go on this trip, in spite of her concerns about being away from him, the Lord began to reveal Himself to Pam in a special way. Pam shares, "It was the first time that I found Scriptures that said that the Lord would be my husband and take care of me. It was the first time that words of prophecy were spoken to me."

The trip to Israel in February of 1977 was the capstone of George's time in California. It was a Bible school like no other. The teaching, the conversations, the times of prayer and worship, the visits to places that had earlier been only words on a page, all worked to further instill in George a love for the Word of God and prophecy, and the hope of the soon return of Jesus. While in Israel, George filmed as many of the places and messages as possible. Years later, George would replay these videos many times with those he was discipling. I personally remember watching these videos with George and seeing the excitement in his eyes, the pages of the Bible opening right before me as I could see the places mentioned in Scripture. Furthermore, to see how God in times past had fulfilled his Word is the guarantee that future prophecies will soon come to pass. "Israel is God's clock," George would often share. "If you want to know where we are at in the grand scheme of history, just look at Israel."

Upon George's return from Israel to southern California, George and Pam knew that their time there was coming to an end. A word of prophecy was spoken over George which confirmed to them that their time at Calvary

Chapel of Costa Mesa was only temporary: "I have taken you from a land of famine to bring you into a land of feasting." Soon after this prophecy was shared, Pastor Chuck gave George a letter requesting that a pastor be sent to lead a congregation in another state. Two weeks before Easter in 1977, the Markeys once again pulled up their tent pegs and departed for Houston, Texas.

EYE CANDY

Knowing that the Lord is leading and knowing where He is leading are two very different things. The Lord had made clear that His plans for George and Pam lay elsewhere. But exactly where, they did not know. This letter from Pastor Chuck and the need in Texas seemed like a good opportunity. So with excitement and anticipation, the Markeys rolled into the great city of Houston.

Upon arriving, George and Pam were immediately impressed. The church was growing, the people were excited, and they had been meeting in a school because of the need for more space. Those who were involved in the body seemed sincere and very kind. The agreement was that George and Pam would stay for a one-month trial, each week living in the home of someone from the church. "These homes were nice, even extravagant," Pam recalls. "We were shocked at the wealth of the community and the people who were coming." George led a Sunday-morning service and a midweek Bible study. The church leaders had already picked out a home that they were going to give to the Markeys. Understanding that they would be financially well provided for by the church, Pam began to feel that this could be a good place to settle down and raise a family.

SQUARE PEG, ROUND HOLE

However, as George and Pam continued to live with the people in their homes, serve in the church, and seek the Lord concerning the plans that He had for their family, it became clear that something was just not right. "In the end, George just didn't feel that it was right for us. There were differences of opinion between George and the leaders on some issues concerning leadership and men in the church. Really, if we were going to stay, things would have to change." Pam was hesitant, but George met with the men of the church and told them what he thought. In matters concerning the health and welfare of the church, George was not known for tact. He knew the Word of God, he knew his calling, and he knew that he would not be able to serve this body in the manner in which it was being led. Before their trial month in Houston was even finished, George decided that it was time to go. "Why should we stay if this is not what the Lord wants?" George asked. Disappointed, yet grateful, they made plans to leave.

CHAPTER ELEVEN

BACK HOME AGAIN IN INDIANA

It WAS ANOTHER ONE of those moments. A decision had been made to leave in obedience to the Lord, but the next place was not yet known. Ideas and opinions swirled around in the car as they were driving out of Houston. Perhaps it would be best to head back to California and wait for another church that was looking for a pastor? Maybe, but that just didn't seem right. They knew that the Lord had given them that time at Calvary Chapel of Costa Mesa, but they also knew that He had directed them to leave. With no other options before them, they decided to head back to central Indiana, visit with friends and family, and work until the Lord showed them otherwise. It would be soon, after all, that they would get another letter and they would be on their way. Or at least that is what they thought. As the van pulled into Ladoga, Indiana, in the summer of 1977, little did they know that what they thought would be only a temporary stopover would turn into more than a decade of rich relationships, exciting ministry, and times of joy and sorrow.

Another letter sent and the same answer received: "Start something where you are," Pastor Chuck wrote back. Brooding over this reply, George retorted to Pam, "He does not know what it is like here. This is not California." Expecting to be in the Midwest for only a short time, George and Pam chose not to move back to their family's farmhouse, which was being leased out. Instead, they rented a small house on the nearby farm of George's previous discipler, Lester Swoverland.

During this time of waiting, fully ready to move at a moment's notice, George got a job on another farm tending sheep. A shepherd. After all, that's what he was preparing to be. As he waited on the Lord to give him a flock of people to shepherd, George now had an opportunity to get a little taste of what it could be like. Sheep. George would learn many biblical illustrations during his time of sheep-herding. However, as he observed the farmer and learned how to properly tend a flock, George continued thinking that he should be somewhere else. He would soon see that a halfhearted and unknowing shepherd is one who could unwittingly permit the introduction of many problems.

George shared the following story from his experiences on this farm. "One time the farmer that I was working for had to leave on a trip. As I was tending to the sheep, I soon began to notice that some of them had runny noses. The next day I went out and those sheep were dead. You see, sheep are really weak animals. One day they can have a little runny nose, and the next day they can just fall over, dead. By the time the farmer returned, I had stacked up a large pile of dead sheep." George continued, "In life, just like those sheep we are susceptible to infection, and in need of the attentive care of a loving shepherd. One who knows us and can see the warning signs of something harmful that could destroy us and those around us." Jesus said, "I am the good shepherd. The good shepherd gives His life for the sheep. But a hireling, he who is not the shepherd, one who does not own the sheep, sees the wolf coming and leaves the sheep and flees; and the wolf catches the sheep and scatters them. The hireling flees because he is a hireling and does not care about the sheep. I am the good shepherd; and I know My sheep, and am known by My own." (John 10:11-14)

Furthermore, George learned that sheep can become stressed or anxious when separated from a flock, and thus more prone to accident or vulnerable to predation. Sheep function best when they are a part of a good flock, with a loving shepherd. In our day of independence, for many it is tempting and even seems good to choose a boundless freedom to the supposed constraining atmosphere of a church. The question is often asked, "Why do I need the church? Why can't I just study the Bible, worship, and pray by myself?" The answer, of course, is that you can. George believed that, just as a flock does not make one a sheep, so the Body of Christ does not make one a Christian. But the Lord has placed us into the Body of Christ, and specifically into a local body, not for our restriction or limitation, but for our good, for the good of others, and for His glory. On this the Bible is clear, and George always stressed the importance of being an active part of a local church, warts and all. "And let us consider one another in order to stir up love and good works, not forsaking the assembling of ourselves together, as is the manner of some, but exhorting one another, and so much the more as you see the Day approaching" (Heb. 10:24-25).

George also shared of his experiences in herding sheep. "One time I was supposed to load a truck with sheep that were headed to market. I spent a long time trying to drive the sheep into that truck. I yelled at the sheep, beat the sheep, pulled, and kicked them. Finally, when I could not figure out what to do, the farmer told me to take one sheep and carry it into the truck, and then to get out of the way. I did what he said and could hardly get out of the way before all those sheep rushed into the back of that truck." Sheep can be easily led when they are given an example. We are also looking for examples, role models, heroes, those who will go before us and show us the way. Too many pastors and churches use the law in attempts to control, drive, and even manipulate the people. In writing to pastors, the Apostle Peter gives the following charge: "Shepherd the flock of God which is among you, serving as overseers, not by compulsion but willingly, not for dishonest gain but eagerly; nor as being lords over those entrusted to you, but being examples to the flock; and when the Chief Shepherd appears, you will receive the crown of glory that does not fade away" (I Pet. 5:2-4).

"Sheep are so dumb that they can get lost going around the corner of a barn," George said. "And you know what? God says that we are like sheep. Now, I think that's funny." Above all, it is important to know the voice of the Shepherd. Sheep are very good at distinguishing voices around them. Jesus said, "My sheep hear My voice and I know them and they follow me" (John 10:27). With all of the voices screaming for our attention in this world, it is crucial that we discern the One voice that matters above all other voices.

The lessons learned during this time would stay with George for the rest of his life. They would become not only additional signposts pointing back to God's faithfulness, care, and timing, but also teaching tools through which he could better tend God's sheep. Forged in the fire, George's faith was tempered in times of chaos, despair, and discouragement. His character became clearly visible as he routinely turned to the Lord to be his high tower, provider, and Great Shepherd. More often than not, the Lord takes times of struggle, periods of unknown, to mold us into the people He wants us to be.

Not a naturally patient man, George was eager to get involved in what the Lord had for them next. Working, waiting, wondering. It was a difficult time for George and Pam as they waited upon the Lord for direction. "We had not found a church to attend, but we would read the Word and try to encourage each other," remembers Pam. "We would also get together a couple of times a week with George's classmate and study the Bible. Other than that, we were just biding our time, not really thinking of starting something there," says Pam. As time went on, however, other matters came to George's attention that required his consideration, and that also kept them in the area longer than they had planned.

DAYS OF DECEIT

Some years earlier, in October of 1973, while George and Pam had been living in Portsmouth, Ohio, George's father, William, had passed way. Edgar S. Husted was a famous lawyer and partner in one of the oldest and most respected law firms in the area. A man of great reputation and from a well-known family, Husted was an attorney who was often retained for the disbursements of family trusts and estates. He was also treasurer for several organizations, and was active in serving the community. Husted was the attorney chosen to represent the interests of the Markey family after the death of their father.

Now that George and Pam were living in the area, George began going through his father's records and accounts. Soon he realized that something didn't add up. "I think George was first suspicious of the low dollar amount listed by Husted for grain receipts," shares Rhonda, George's sister. "George went to the grain elevators, and they confirmed that the figures were very low." As executor of his father's estate, George continued to dig and began to discover other financial inconsistencies that had resulted in the losses of tens of thousands of dollars from the family. Rhonda recalls, "I'm not sure at what point we realized that our signature cards at the bank had been forged by Husted, but the thefts and forgery were now obvious."

After checking and rechecking his figures, George finally approached the authorities and reported the crimes. "No one wanted to believe me," George said. "Everyone felt that Husted was such an honorable man and that it was impossible for him to be guilty of a crime." So George continued to gather information.

I am not sure when George first acquired the nickname "Columbo," after the famous TV detective, but George often had a demeanor that would give one the impression that he didn't know anything when in reality he had all of the pieces already put together in his mind. As George began to investigate Edgar Husted, he soon realized that they were not the only family who had been affected. "He had stolen from people before us who didn't say anything because Husted's father paid them off," discloses Rhonda. "We didn't think it would be fair to others to let this get swept under the rug, even if they [the Husted family] could pay us. This wasn't just a one-time thing." A newspaper clipping from that time writes, "Although Husted is accused of misappropriating funds from as many as a dozen clients over the past 5½ years, only Markey has been willing to press charges."

"The judge who tried the case was almost blind," recalled George of special Judge Robert Hall. George continued, "And when the sentence was given, he came down hard on Husted, saying, 'You may have fooled most of the people in this courtroom and in the community into feeling sorry for you, but I see through your show of words." Interestingly, another judge, Judge Sommer, who years earlier had told George in court that his life would never amount to anything, testified on behalf of Husted and said that he should receive a suspended sentence. "Husted was a con man who had fooled the whole community, but they didn't want to admit that they had been taken," George said.

March 24, 1979: Headlines concerning the standing-room-only trial read, "Husted Details $313,000 Theft." In handing down the maximum sentences, Judge Hall said, "Most of the people you have taken advantage of were people you were involved with after the death of someone, people who had been injured in accidents, people who were over 65 or were incompetent... It would be a farce of the system of justice if an individual such as you does not suffer the consequences the legislature has set out for this offense." Husted was sent to serve out his time at the Rockville Rehabilitation

Center. Subsequent trials of Edgar S. Husted have even made it into the law books. Upon Husted's release, George discovered that he was continuing to swindle people. One lady in the congregation that George later pastored in Crawfordsville was coaxed into paying for his vacations to Alaska.

George's faith was deepened through this time. "It is terrible when someone you trust steals from you," said resident Mike Mutterspaugh concerning this situation. "But George was able to give it over to the Lord." However, for George, "giving something over to the Lord" included being obedient to expose the evil so that others would not be affected. Had George remained quiet, the injustices would not have abated. As the famous saying attributed to Edmund Burke states, "All that is needed for evil to triumph is for good men to do nothing."

George had a strong sense of right and wrong, justice and injustice. He frequently favored the underdog and rose to challenge violations against individuals and groups. He stood for moral, righteous causes and was appalled at the apathy of people who would not stand up for what was right. In our time of tolerance and indifference, George Markey was one of a dying breed of brave, vocal men. Not content to let unrighteousness go unanswered, soon after the trial of Husted George and his sister Rhonda continued to hold demonstrations in front of the bank associated with Husted's crimes. The bank would not claim responsibility in any way for the widespread losses in the area, but the publicity generated through these events would not be forgotten in the community.

On another occasion, George would lead volunteers from the church in Crawfordsville in a protest against a local Holiday Inn that had scheduled a performance of the male strip group the Chippendales. He wasn't about to sit back and let them come into town with their skewed morals. In fact, when he found out about it, George said, "Not on my watch." He then got people to make signs, and everyone picketed in front of the hotel. Later attempts to have the Chippendales at a bar in downtown Crawfordsville resulted in similar protests. Friend and fellow protester LaRhonda Zachary said, "We didn't obstruct the entrance and we didn't yell at passersby; in fact, the people [who supported the Chippendales] didn't want to be seen." As a result of the protests, the group had only one performance in town and then never came back.

On yet another occasion, George heard that members of the Ku Klux Klan (KKK) were going to be marching in downtown Crawfordsville. Appalled at the continued toleration of segregation, racism, and violence by many in the community, George took this as an opportunity to march against the KKK in order to show his repulsion for their views. However, George's high morals, opinions, and open resistance to something that many people still supported, unfortunately even Christians, would turn out to be used against him in the future.

CHAPTER TWELVE

12

THE BEGINNINGS
IN NEW ROSS

IN THE SOVEREIGN plan of God, these days of deceit were one of the obstacles that kept George and Pam in Indiana longer than they had anticipated. As time passed, George and Pam became more rooted in the area. Their relationships with people, roles in the community, and responsibilities in taking care of friends and loved ones continued to grow. Pam, always busy with the twins and now pregnant with their third child, was also taking care of Betty Swoverland, who was bedridden. Pam shares, "I would take the twins over to the house to care for her since she could not get out of bed on her own." When asked about Mrs. Swoverland's demeanor, Pam replies, "She was still a bitter woman. Yes, she believed in the Lord, knew all the right things about grace, but was never a happy lady herself, especially when she was in pain. It was a real strain to be there with the twins, trying to keep them quiet." But in spite of the challenges, Pam continued to serve Betty, realizing that it brought Betty some comfort and also freed up Les, not only for work, but also for continued discipleship with George. Lester Swoverland became "Grandpa Les" to the twins, always his generous, gracious self, and once again was spending quality time with George in the Word.

Two weeks before the birth of their third child, George and Pam decided that it was time to move back into the old farmhouse. The renters had left and it needed to be fixed up. "The farmhouse was a mess," Pam recounts. "Trash was everywhere. And there were rats, big rats. They would keep trying to take our potatoes. They were very big rats." Not wanting to poison the rats for fear of having the lingering smell in the house, George would stay up at night with a baseball bat and a rifle. "The rats would hide, even standing up on their back feet behind the washing machine," George shared. "I had quite a time getting rid of them."

The call came on the same night that Pam went into labor. The elders from the church where George had gotten saved years earlier were wanting to meet with George. They had recently lost their pastor and were wondering whether George would agree to be interim pastor as they continued to search for a replacement. George agreed to the temporary position, making sure that they knew that he was not planning to be there for long. Later that same night, in May of 1978, George drove Pam to the hospital in Crawfordsville, where their new baby daughter, Robin, was born.

The church in New Ross was an old, traditional church. Upon walking up the steps and entering the sanctuary, one could see the wooden plaque on the wall listing both the number of people in attendance and the total amount given in tithes and offerings from the previous Sunday service. In front of the pulpit lay the large Bible, untouched, unmoved, unused, but a testimony to the importance of tradition. George and Pam, both nontraditional and nonconformist, began loving and serving this small body of believers. "I began singing some of the new, fresh praise choruses," remembers Pam. Unfamiliar with anything other than the songs listed in the hymnal, the people listened with delight to the new songs, but, for the most part, did not participate themselves. One of the first things that George did as interim pastor was to take down the tithe and attendance plaque. "Why would people want to advertise the fact that people gave $58 last week?" George inquired. Although there was resistance to some of the changes, many people began coming to the church.

"There were two fruitful things that came out of our time in New Ross," Pam relates. "The first was a midweek Bible study that took place behind the sanctuary. In fact, there were more people coming to that Bible study than to the Sunday-morning service. The second was a women's Bible study. People were coming who were so hungry for spiritual things." At the time George and Pam returned to the Midwest, there already had been some pockets of spiritual renewal among various groups there as well. But, as is always the case, counterfeit revivals frequently come alongside something genuine, and the true power of the Holy Spirit to change a person is replaced with an exalting of the flesh. As the women would come to the Bible studies, Pam remembers them asking questions about religious programs they had seen on TV. "For a whole year I would listen to them talk about these preachers, and I never would speak out against them. I would just say, 'Well, what does the Bible say?' But one day I decided to watch one of the programs. The next time we got together the ladies began asking me about such and such a preacher, and I answered, 'You know, we have been studying the Bible straight through, in context. What does this guy do? And the ladies began to see the difference."

Then it happened. One Sunday George came to church, closed the big traditional Bible, and put it down on a lower shelf under the pulpit. "You would have thought that I had threatened the life of someone," George said. "But all I wanted to do was to preach from my own Bible." Another board meeting was called and the matter discussed. However, with George having grown up in this community and having a reputation as the local rebel, people almost seemed to expect this of him. For George, "status quo" was basically a sin. He was not going to maintain the normal state of affairs just because "that is how we have always done it." Yet he was not a rebel just for the sake of being a rebel. George's preeminent desire was that people would have a living relationship with Jesus, not built on any tradition of man. Furthermore, he knew that the young people were being turned off by the hypocrisy of their parents around him, smug in their religiosity on Sundays yet shedding any remnants of a godly example upon exiting the church doors.

It was always on George's heart to see young people involved in the church, and the youth were not coming. "He was always talking to young people on the streets," shares Diana Rogers Faulk, who worked at the nearby grain elevator. As the daughter of a local farmer and one who had attended the same high school as George, Diana knew George and had witnessed the change in his life. "He used to come back from Bible college and hold revival meetings in our church, playing the piano and preaching. He brought joy into our church." In her encounters with George and Pam, Diana's life was revolutionized by the grace of God. She began fellowshiping frequently at home with the Markeys, besides attending the church there in New Ross. However, out of concern for her son and daughter, George actually suggested to Diana that she find another church – "somewhere where the youth are going." George was not seeking to build a kingdom, but he had a heart for people, especially for young people, desiring to see them in a place where they could grow spiritually.

The time of leading the church in New Ross lasted for almost one and a half years, up until the birth of their fourth child, Rhonda, in December of 1979. It was at this time that someone else in the church was finally ready to take over the pastorate of this congregation. In Pam's words, "The people at the church in New Ross were a sweet and kind people." In retrospect, it is interesting to see how God used this church during such pivotal points in the life of George: when he was saved, sending him to Bible college, receiving him on return visits, permitting him to be interim pastor while awaiting God's next call on his life, and later, even in assisting George and his family in taking the Gospel to other nations. What may have appeared to George and Pam as an inflexible, traditional group of people was a divine instrument of God's love.

AN OPPORTUNITY

No visit to Crawfordsville, Indiana, is complete without a tour of the Lew Wallace study. Famous for his role as a commanding officer during the Civil War, General Wallace was also a lawyer, a politician, a statesman, and an author. His historical novel Ben-Hur: A Tale of the Christ, has been called "the most influential Christian book of the nineteenth century." Free public showings of the movie adapted from the book, starring Charlton Heston, were an annual tradition at the old Strand Theater in Crawfordsville during the Easter season.

It was in the spring of 1980 when George and Pam were sitting in the Strand Theater watching Ben-Hur. "George knew everybody," says Pam. "And if he didn't know someone, then he would go up, introduce himself, and find out about them." After the movie, George began talking with a couple seated in front of them. "What are you doing on Sunday?" the couple inquired of George and Pam. Having just left the church in New Ross, the Markeys had been attending various churches in the area, but had not yet found a church they could call home. They could not find any place that taught systematically through the Bible, something very important to George. As they stood in the Strand movie theater, it was decided that the two families would get together out at George and Pam's farmhouse the following Sunday in order to study the Bible, fellowship, and pray.

At the end of the meeting that next Sunday, the question was posed by the couple, "Well, do you want to do this again?" George's response: "Sure, I guess so." And so it was, over the course of the next year, that the Markeys' old farmhouse near Ladoga became a new house-church in the community. Sunday after Sunday new people and families would show up. Soon the farmhouse was packed. Alan and LaRhonda Zachary were some of the first ones to come to these meetings. "I came from a strict, denominational background and Alan was from a small traditional church," shares LaRhonda. "These meetings at George and Pam's were very, very different than what I was used to. I started telling my momma about it, about the music and how he just teaches right out of the Bible. With a gasp she would say, 'You don't sing hymns?' Or, 'Is he even ordained?'" LaRhonda continues, "Well, my parents came to visit one day and we took them with us to the farmhouse. Once they met George and Pam they felt a lot different about where we were going to church—their questions and skepticism were laid to rest."

Why another church in the Bible Belt? George's heart had always been to go to those places where there was an obvious need. "I just want to go where people are open to hear," George had said. "I am tired of sharing with a fence post." Could there actually be a spiritual openness in one of the most religious places in the country? Some years ago I researched the presence of at least 104 congregations in Montgomery County, at a time when the population of the county was about 35,000 people—definitely a very religious community. George longed to see a genuine, spiritual response, a zeal for the Lord, a change in the hearts of people that would revolutionize how they lived, not just bodies filling pews. Could that even happen here?

A MODEL

As the fellowship of believers continued to grow and mature, it became obvious that this group could become the core of a new church. Always sensing the importance of showing people a model, George decided to take a group of people to a Calvary Chapel Conference that was taking place in

Pennsylvania. Over the course of the next few years, George would take several groups of people to participate in these conferences, which were led by Chuck Smith, Raul Ries, Gayle Erwin, Don McClure, and other leaders and teachers in the Calvary Chapel movement.

In writing his last letter to Timothy, the Apostle Paul mentions terms like "pattern," "the things you have heard," "the things you have learned," "you have carefully followed," and other words and phrases that show the importance of observing a model, an example. Also, in the book of Philippians Paul writes, "Brethren, join in following my example, and note those who so walk, as you have us for a pattern... The things which you learned and received and heard and saw in me, these do, and the God of peace will be with you." (Phil. 3:17; 4:9) "George was big on the model," Pam shared. "He wanted people to see a model." George wanted people to see for themselves a work of the Spirit, not just to take his word for it. However, whether people actually saw and understood what George wanted them to see and understand is a different question.

In my conversations with people who went on these trips to Pennsylvania with George, I have yet to hear any comments about the teaching or teachers there. Not to say that the teaching wasn't good, but rather the comments that I hear have been almost solely about George. It is one thing to hear a teaching, but it is something completely different to see it lived out right in front of your eyes. LaRhonda Zachary recalls one of these trips: "I remember going to Pennsylvania. There was a huge group of us. Of course, there were no cell phones at that time, so we could not call ahead. We pulled into this little restaurant to eat, and all of us went in. There was only one waitress, and as she looked at us you could see the whites of her eyes. George went over to her and introduced himself, saying, 'Ma'am, I know we are a big group; can you handle us? We'll help you. We'll do whatever is needed.' It was amazing. We rearranged the entire room. She stepped out of the way and George was right there at the lead. 'Move this.' 'Put those tables over there.' 'Turn the tables this way.' 'Let's sit like this.' And then, everyone sat down—everyone except George. He got up and started serving water. He was passing out menus. He took our orders. He was helping this waitress. He was up, literally, serving us. So often when you see the leader of a group, he is there to be served. Someone else should get up and do the helping. Not George.

And of course, with George up there serving, others got up and started helping. And that is how he taught servant leadership. By doing it."

FINDING A CHURCH HOME

The Ladoga farmhouse was soon too small to hold everyone who was coming on Sundays. In the summer, the group would often meet in the city park, staying long after the service was over for "pitch-ins" and fellowship. It was decided that the name of their new fellowship would be "Christ Fellowship." Articles of Incorporation for Christ Fellowship were signed by George and Pam, dated, and approved on June 8, 1981. A later amendment to the Articles of Incorporation reflected the change of the name of the church to "Calvary Chapel of Crawfordsville, Inc." Over the next couple of years, this growing group of believers would meet at places such as the Methodist church, a daycare center called "Littleville," and a strip mall on the east side of town. Baby Melanie, their fifth child, became the new addition to the growing Markey family while the church was meeting at the strip mall in October of 1981.

"We were looking for any place to get in out of the rain," LaRhonda remembers. Eventually finding a site on the edge of town called "The Sportsmen's Club," the young congregation began meeting there sometime in 1983. With places to swim and fish, and open fields for sports and picnics, The Sportsmen's Club provided an excellent place for fellowship. However, the main building on the property that would house the growing church was in poor condition, and the group immediately set about making repairs. LaRhonda adds, "Everyone was pitching in. It was real dirty, sooty. There had probably been some kind of fire there in the past. There was a lot of painting and cleaning going on. Everyone donated furniture, carpets, and rugs." Soon after the church began meeting in The Sportsmen's Club, little David was born in July of 1983—child number six.

That same month, George took a group with him from the church to a Calvary Chapel radio rally that was taking place in Indianapolis. Pastor Chuck Smith and other leaders of the movement were present. The evening before the rally was to begin, to the surprise of George and Pam, Pastor Chuck announced at a dinner that they were recognizing what God was doing in and through George and were ordaining him as a pastor in the Calvary Chapel movement. The leaders gathered around George, laid hands on him, and prayed for him. The next morning at the rally, Pastor Chuck called George up to the front and publicly prayed for him, reaffirming the ordination from the previous evening. In one of George's last messages, he spoke of this time of ministry and life. "God calls us, but often it is a question of God's timing. When will it be realized? Often, it is years. In the meantime we are learning how to trust the Lord, how to be faithful." Referencing D. L. Moody, George remarked that just as the Lord took 40 years to teach Moses that he was a nobody, so it was in his life. "I was 40 years of age when the Lord thrust me into a fruitful ministry, the beginning of the Calvary Chapel in Crawfordsville," George continued. "So God's preparation time may take years, but don't be disappointed if things don't happen right away and you spend years wondering and waiting. Because God is preparing you. He is preparing His servant." In I Corinthians 4:2 Paul writes that the most important aspect of a minister of God is that he or she be faithful. This stability mixed with loyalty, rooted in a deep understanding of God and His Word by a person who is yielded to His will, is the defining mark of a servant of God and is one of the most essential characteristics in a successful servant-leader.

Of this season in the church, LaRhonda shares, "Today, everyone always talks about 'back when.' No wonder we loved each other so much; we were together all the time. All the time. Whether at baptisms or pitch-ins, or women's and men's studies, prayer meetings, or with babies, no wonder we were so close. All of the fellowship together. I remember counting at one point, and from Sunday to Sunday, six out of seven days a week, at least one of us was in a Bible study or a prayer meeting."

Lives were being changed, and lifelong friendships were being made. Mike Abney was a man who had stopped drinking only a couple of years before meeting George. "I was told that I should be around these kind of people," Mike recalls. "I knew that I would go back to alcohol without something. That's how I came to Jesus. And from the time that I met George, I went to church every Sunday, to his Bible study, and to other meetings." Mike soon began roofing with George as well. "We were together every day, and the whole time we were together it involved God's Word." Others who worked with George through the years would testify to the same thing, the preeminent place given to the Word of God. Everywhere George would work, whether roofing, painting, or carpentry, he would take a large portable tape player and have either worship music or teaching tapes playing. During lunch breaks they would sit in George's van and listen to J. Vernon McGee, John MacArthur, Chuck Swindoll, Charles Stanley, or other solid Bible teachers on the radio. But for Mike, most of what he learned was from George himself. "He was the first person in my life who, when he said something, it went in my ears and stayed there," remembers Mike. "He was teaching something that was real. That is what captured my attention, and his love. He knew how to love me. George had a gentleness about him that I did not understand. He touched people's hearts. This attracted us and caused people to listen."

The model not only was being shown, but now was being reproduced. As George had been affected by the grace of God, filled with the Spirit of God, and shown examples through the godly lives of his mentors, others began to crave this spiritual reality in their own lives. This reality was neither a brand of Christianity nor a form of religiosity. Rather it was a personal relationship with the only One who could breathe new life into people where sin, darkness, and death had previously reigned. As Mike Abney and countless others discovered, this life was transforming; this God, amazing! What followed for George were many years of patiently explaining and transmitting this vision that he had received to the people whom he was called to serve.

CHAPTER THIRTEEN

THE VISION
OF GEORGE

"A MAN OF VISION" is a phrase that many people use in describing George. Through the seasons of George's early life, his salvation, his discipleship, his struggles in college, his years in Portsmouth, and the time in California, God was preparing His servant, but He also was instilling in George a vision to communicate and demonstrate to His people. For the most part, those in the Midwest had never heard of teaching through the Bible, chapter by chapter, verse by verse. They had not witnessed servant leadership to the extent that they saw it portrayed in George. Church was basically a traditional obligation that was fulfilled on Sunday rather than a dynamic relationship affecting one's complete life. As grace had revolutionized George's life, as he had been filled with the Holy Spirit and had been witness to times of revival, so he wanted to see the lives of others affected in similar ways. He was a man of vision in the sense that he knew what he wanted to see in the Body of Christ, and would not be satisfied until it happened. A leader without vision from God cannot properly direct the people of God, nor can he effectively communicate the Word of God to the people of God. Day by day, meeting by meeting, George was imparting the vision he had received in both word and action to a growing number of people. It was the vision of a body reaching in, a body reaching out, and a body reaching up.

A BODY REACHING IN

The Word of God is both living and active, sharper than any two-edged sword (Heb. 4:12). Wherever the Word of God is taught, received, and acted on, it brings transformation. As the Word of God was being taught in home Bible studies, during Sunday and mid-week services, or over cups of coffee at a local restaurant, people were changing. One of the primary evidences for a work of God is an increased love for the family of God. As George often said, "The greatest compliment that anyone can say about this church is that they see love here." The Apostle John wrote, "By this all will know that you are My disciples, if you have love for one another" (John 13:35). The desire for being together, being in the Word, and being in corporate prayer is a common testimony on the lips of many who attended Calvary Chapel of Crawfordsville.

THE APOSTLES' DOCTRINE

One who always gave place to the Word of God, George sought to instill in his congregation and its leadership a love for the Word. Various speakers from around the country would be invited to give special teachings or weekend seminars on how to study the Bible inductively—to observe, interpret, and apply. George also encouraged Bible studies and home fellowships to begin, apart from his own involvement in them. In fact, in my own life I found that the greatest time of growth in my early Christian experience was when I began attending a Friday-night Bible study, which George never attended himself, but wholeheartedly supported.

Jim Spencer is a teacher and pastor who was a part of Calvary Chapel of Crawfordsville early on. Jim shares, "George was fairly protective of his pulpit and rarely allowed others to occupy it. I never felt that was motivated by any fear or jealousy but simply by his commitment to see that the Word was properly divided. Once a year I was allowed to fill the Sunday pulpit when George took half the congregation to the Ichthus Festival in Kentucky. When I asked him if there was anything in particular that he wanted me to preach, he would smile and say, 'Why don't you talk about giving?' When I asked why he wanted me to do that, he explained, 'The same reason the doctor has the nurse give you the shot.'"

BREAKING OF BREAD

George was not interested in beating the sheep, weighing them down with guilt, but rather felt the express call of a shepherd to lead them to green pastures, to flowing waters, that they would be growing in the love of

God. From pitch-ins to all-night prayer meetings, and from conferences to concerts, these close times of loving fellowship developed an intense sense of unity among the body. Food is one thing that unites all of us. Everyone has to eat. In George's mind it was always "Why not just do it together?" Whether through hog roasts and pitch-ins at the church, or leading a mass exodus of people to the local Wendy's restaurant after the Sunday service, George was always encouraging people to spend time together. He just loved being with people, serving them, and enjoying a good laugh around the table. The more tables that had to be put together to fit everyone, the better.

George would often point out that Jesus also seems to have been particularly fond of fellowship around a table of good food. Whether He is eating with tax collectors and sinners or teaching His disciples by washing their feet before dinner, much of the Jesus we see in the Gospels is in the setting of a meal or a festivity. Even after His resurrection from the dead, Jesus proves His reality to his disciples by sharing a meal with them. Furthermore, at the end of time when we are with Jesus face to face, He tells us in the Book of Revelation that to those who overcome, He will give to eat from the tree of life and from the hidden manna (Rev. 2:7,17).

PRAYERS

"You can tell if a church is healthy by looking at its prayer meeting," George frequently said. Although George never considered himself to be a model in the area of prayer, he was one who would frequently encourage others to pray. George knew that the key to any work of God was a reliance on God, and what better way to express one's reliance on God than through prayer. Another public school teacher and pastor, Glen McFarland, shares about the Monday-night men's prayer meeting at Calvary Chapel. "I recall seeing the power of prayer when the men prayed. Just witnessing those guys believing that it could happen was amazing. In some cases we would quit the prayer meetings early to go visit someone who had come up in prayer."

Jim Spencer remembers, "When I asked George how to teach men to pray, he smiled and said, 'Just get together and pray.'" He continues, "One of my favorite memories is seeing George walk into a gathering of men, sit down on the floor, take off his boots, and say, 'Let's pray!' I even remember a few of us asking George what he thought it would be like to pray all night. 'Let's find out,' George said. 'How about Friday at your house, Jim?' We gave it our best shot, and I can still see Jamie Menard asleep on the couch while the rest of us tried to work our way through our fourth pot of coffee."

George was always excited to minister to the spiritual needs of those in the congregation. One occasion that everyone seems to remember is the winter that the "number one drug dealer in town" got saved. With an immediate desire to part with his previous lifestyle, he approached George after the service and asked him whether he would baptize him. George answered, "Sure, as soon as it warms up." Not wanting to delay, this man persisted and said that he wanted to be baptized now. Although the ice on the pond near the church was four inches thick, George agreed and the church marched down to the pond. As the congregation stood shivering under blankets on the beach, George proceeded to cut a hole in the ice with a hatchet. The two of them went in and George baptized him. LaRhonda Zachary remembers, "It was probably the only baptism where George didn't ask if there was anyone else who wanted to be baptized."

FELLOWSHIP

George also was responsible for beginning the Calvary Chapel Midwest Pastors Conference, which continues to this day. With his heart desiring to see fellowship between the churches, as well as a closer place for people to come and see a model of what God could do, George began looking for ways to get something started locally. Gayle Erwin remembers, "George approached me about the conference and he said, 'Who do I have to see about starting a conference here?' I said, 'You don't have to see anybody; you just do it.' He was a bit shocked at that because he figured that there had to be something official. I said, 'Oh no, all of these conferences started on their own.' So George asked, 'Well, if we try to start one here, would you partner with me?' George soon began the conference at the nearby Fellowship of Christian Athletes conference center, and Gayle supplied the guest speakers. "We outgrew that conference center long before we left it," Gayle adds. "People were sitting in windows and such, and then it moved to just outside of Hartford City."

George always emphasized unity, and not just among the believers in his own fellowship or other Calvary Chapel churches. Early on in his time of ministry in Crawfordsville, George began organizing weekly men's breakfasts. Men from different denominations would come together at six in the morning in order to study the Word of God, openly share their hearts, and pray for one another. Dick Van Arsdel is a professional educator and member of the First Baptist Church who began attending these gatherings early on. He shares, "I think we were in that Bible study for 15 years. When I first went to the Bible study, I was hesitant because I had heard of these charismatic people. I was a little bit unsure of wanting to get involved with those kinds." Dick's first meeting with George was the time when his defenses were torn away. He remembers, "This man gave me a bear hug like he did everybody. I thought that he was going to crush every bone in my body. There never was a simple handshake, and I never forgot his bear hug."

For Dick, and the many other men who attended this early-morning Bible study, the lessons they learned from George were not just through his teachings, but even more so from his life. Dick recalls the following: "George taught me what real grace was and that grace was free and that there was nothing that I could do. He started out by buying my breakfast, and I'd say, 'Well, I get yours next week.' And the next week he'd buy my breakfast. And I said, 'You've got to quit this. I'll get my own and I'd like to buy yours.' And until I could say 'thank you' and never say another word, I kept getting free breakfasts. Finally, George looked at me square in the eyes and said, 'Dick, just remember that Jesus paid the price for you to have eternal life. There is nothing that you can do. You cannot repay him, you cannot get even with him or anything else. It is free, Dick, and when you can accept this breakfast as free, then I'll quit buying.' It was his way of teaching me that Jesus' gift was free and that it was an unearned and an undeserved gift. And I saw him do that with other guys. It's our nature to resist grace, but he just drove that point home. Sometimes teachers like me can be bullheaded."

From teachers and engineers to former alcoholics and high-school dropouts, men from all over the county, from various denominations, would come together to study the Word and seek the Lord. In times of drought they would gather to pray in the center of Crawfordsville, or come together on the streets of Ladoga to seek the Lord for revival. In fact, those special weekly men's gatherings continue to this day. Like George, I am convinced that if and when revival comes, it will come through groups of men like this who come together to pray regardless of denominational ties.

A BODY REACHING OUT

One thing George never wanted to be a part of was a church that was focused only on itself. A body reaching in to one another is good only if this is done with the express intent of equipping the saints and building up one another for the purpose of reaching out to those who do not know Jesus. Having come to the Lord through someone sharing the Gospel message with him at work, and having cut his spiritual teeth under the tutelage of men like Lester Swoverland, Chuck Smith, and his missionary father-in-law, John Pemberton, George had a burning passion to share Jesus with those who did not know Him.

EVANGELISM

Jim Spencer shares, "Pastor George taught me early on that evangelism is at the very heart of church life. The excitement of church meetings always comes from new believers. I was always impressed at how George would manage to bring the question of salvation into almost every conversation he was involved in. I can still hear him asking the kid who was bagging our groceries if he knew the Lord, and George pulling into the Target parking lot on a summer Saturday evening to talk with a crowd of bored teenagers about the Lord. I always felt that part of his zeal for evangelism came with the missionary spirit which was a big part of his calling. It finally came into full bloom when the whole Markey family moved to Ukraine."

George always had his Bible with him, driving with it on the dashboard of his van. Conversations would always turn to Scripture, relationships, and evangelism. Whether it was in reaching out to men in state and federal prisons, or to youth in the area, or in supporting missions around the world, George led the charge in sharing Jesus, and he always kept this vision of sharing Jesus before the people.

Close family friend and co-worker Pastor Tom Camp recalls meeting George, and immediately seeing in him a kindred spirit. "My ministry is more like George's: to ex-convicts, to druggies, to the down-and-outers. So when I saw George, I fell in love." Tom remembers what he calls his "George-in-the-van time," just being with George wherever he was going. "He would speak at places, and I would go with him. Whether it was to outreaches, men's meetings, prison work, or just driving around meeting with people."

MINISTRY "TO THE LEAST OF THESE"

The men of Calvary Chapel, under George's leadership, were involved in ministries at places like the Pendleton prison, the Indiana Boys School, the Westville prison, the Indiana State Farm, and other correctional facilities. Tom shares, "The prisoners loved George. Here was this big, burly man who would say, 'Hey!' and give them a bear hug that would disarm them. They had thought that they were bad and tough." Some of these trips would last all day: George and the men would arrive early, walk and talk with the prisoners during the day, and spend time studying the Bible at night. Tom emphasizes, "We just taught the Word of God, not some 'How to Succeed' class or 'How to Get out of Prison' course."

Recalling a story from one of their visits to a prison, Tom shares, "One time after we had been sharing with the prisoners for a few months, they asked if we could have a communion service together. So we brought in juice and bread, and the guards let us through. The prison chaplain would not come—he was kind of a drunk. So we used his communion cups and held the service. Later we received an official letter saying that we had twenty-one counts of trafficking against us. We went back to the prison and talked with the chaplain. He was trying to intimidate us, showing us all of his degrees and credentials. He began asking us for our credentials, and we would answer that 'we just love Jesus.' This went on for a while. Then he would leave the room and come back looking red in the face and a little slurred in his speech, because he was hitting the bottle. He would say, 'I know why you are here. You don't have anywhere else to play your music,' or, 'There must be problems in your church, that's why you have to come here.' Finally, George looked at this chaplain and firmly said, 'Are you ready to hear what I have to say? We're here because we love these men. You don't love these men.'"

Tom Camp and the many other men who rode and served with George repeatedly mention the influence that George had on their lives. "One of the reasons that I feel why I am in the ministry today is because George took me in and believed in me," Tom relates. "Any ministry I would do, George would go there. He was there for me. He went to bat for me when no one else did." George's love and personal interest in the individual, their walk with the Lord, and their family, was instrumental in building up, equipping, and encouraging them so that they could effectively reach out and serve others. Tom remembers, "If my car was not working, George would call the elders to see if the church had enough money to help fix it. When we went out to Wendy's after church, he would not even eat until he made sure people had enough money to buy their own lunch. He would clean things up that people spilled, and would get napkins or straws for people. He was a servant. I have never met anybody like that."

Dick Van Arsdel adds, "He was a mentor. He was an encourager. He was an individual that called you to accountability just by your association with him in that you knew how strong his stance was, and if you were going to be associated with him you better have a backbone too. He did that not by demanding, but through his teaching and his mannerisms and his presence—by how he lived his life. You demanded it of yourself. At least that is how it affected me."

A SPIRITUAL AWAKENING IN A PUBLIC SCHOOL

In the spring of 1985, on the day of the senior class graduation, 133 out of 139 students in the class gathered for prayer in the front of Southmont High School. Please note, Southmont is a public school. But what took place there that year has been described by some as the tail end of the Jesus people movement, and affected many students for the rest their lives. In the early 1980s, George was frequently called in to substitute teach at Southmont, the public high school south of Crawfordsville. Himself heavily influenced by the factual account of David Wilkerson and Nicky Cruz in the books The Cross and the Switchblade and Run, Baby, Run, George would frequently use these teaching assignments at school as opportunities to read excerpts from these books.

David Wray and Brian Hudson were students at the time and remember having George in class and seeing him in the halls. Brian recalls, "The first time I met George was in eighth or ninth grade. George used to substitute teach, and I remember him because he was the only substitute teacher who would not give us any homework. He always brought in Nicky Cruz's book Run, Baby, Run and would read it to the students in the classes." David Wray remembers seeing George walking in the school halls and himself peering into a class as George was giving a Bible study. In sharing about his first conversation with George, David says, "I got saved right before my senior year of high school, and a friend took me to Calvary Chapel. I remember walking up to George after the service and saying, 'Hi, I'm David. I'm at Southmont, and we need a Bible study.' George replied, 'You're absolutely right.' And so I asked him, 'When can you start?' George replied, 'Why don't you do it and I'll support you?' That was our first conversation in the winter of '84, and in January of '85 Brian Hudson and I started a Bible study at my house." The Bible study swelled from 17 kids in the beginning to well over 100 within only a couple of months. "George led us from the background," Brian adds. "He encouraged us to share openly and boldly."

Brian further describes the work of God at these Bible studies and the impact, not only on the school, but on the community as a whole. "Looking back, there is a special blessing of the Lord that He gives in certain seasons of history. I do believe that we caught the tail wind of the Jesus movement. When it hit at Southmont, it was weird. We would walk into a room packed with kids, and Dave and I would not have any clue as to what we were doing. Often it was as simple as picking up the Bible and reading John 3:16 and people would start crying and want to know how to know Jesus, and then they would invite fifteen people to the study the next week. During my last year of high school, I remember the principal pulled me aside and told me that at the beginning of the year, out of his thirty or thirty-five years of being principal, this senior class was the worst that he had ever seen. But then he confessed he had seen such a dramatic change in the students over the year that he was astounded." Lives transformed, broken hearts mended, and dying faith renewed. Because he had such an influence on David Wray, Brian Hudson, and so many in that school, George was asked by the senior class to give the commencement address at the senior graduation. As always, his message was about Jesus, God's tremendous love for us expressed in the life, death, burial, and resurrection of Jesus. No holding back.

Brian adds, "George was the catalyst in all that happened there. He was the one whom God chose to use for that harvest, in that community. And it didn't stop with Calvary Chapel and Southmont, but it flowed over to other pastors, to families from other churches, and to other ministries. Businesses that had Calvary Chapel people in them were beginning to live for Christ. For some reason, God chose George Markey to be the spearhead of that whole thing. George had a way about him that made people uncomfortable, but even those people whom he made uncomfortable seemed to love him. There were churches that were jealous, and people who thought it was a cult because it was so different than what Crawfordsville had ever seen before. It is always easier to be critical than to be full of the grace of God. The more I look back, I think, 'What an amazing time.' Not a week goes by that I don't think of George and remember those times with deep appreciation and fondness."

David clearly summarizes by saying, "There was an uncommon grace of God on us. I know this because I have ministered in places where that grace was not present. But, overall, I truly think that this was also because of George's influence." David recalls George's willingness to take people like Brian and him under his wing. "We were so unbelievably unpolished. One night Brian Hudson and I went out and baptized each other in Sugar Creek. It was a stormy night with lightning and we jumped in and out of the water as fast as we could, just the two of us. We were sick of this old man, our flesh that was following us around. We thought that maybe if we go get dunked we will sever this thing. Well, we got back in the car, soaking wet (we did it in our full clothes), and we drove to Calvary Chapel and barged in on the men's prayer meeting, yelling, 'Hey, we've been baptized.' And for George to take that stuff in stride, just the tremendous way that he took us in."

George would continue meeting with David and Brian on a regular basis to study the Bible as well as New Testament Greek, and also to just sit and talk through life issues together. They were being built up in the faith and receiving a vision from God for life and ministry, but also George was giving them opportunities to reach out. David shares, "George was a discipler. Whenever he was going to the hospital or to the prisons, he would invite me, or convince me, and take me along with him. I remember whenever we would go out to prisons and things like that, George was always the last one to eat, and he was always cleaning up people's trays. He was like a waiter. He was getting people drinks and constantly serving. Those were life-changing memories."

Brian adds, "I never met a man who loved Christ more single-heartedly than George Markey. His vision was a fixed vision. I remember one time Tom Camp and I were hanging out with George. Tom and I would always talk about these great things we wanted to do, and George almost zoned out like he was not hearing us. Tom and I were sharing our hearts and all that we wanted to do, and George was saying, 'Yeah, praise the Lord,' but he kept looking out the window. Then I noticed that there was this guy walking down the street and it was clear to me that he was stoned. George finally stopped us talking and pointed out that guy and said, "You know what, that ol' boy needs Jesus," and we said, 'Yeah, he does,' and kept talking about our plans for ministry. George stopped us and said, 'Well, well, let's go tell him.' So he gets out of the old green van, walks up to the guy, and says, 'I just wanted to tell you that somebody loves you. It's Jesus Christ.' And he continued to talk and share with him. He was so single-hearted." Brian, continuing to describe George and his influence, shares that "loving Jesus with sincerity and having an evangelistic spirit were what I learned most from George. Looking at people and not seeing them as a conquest. A lot of people have the notch-on-the-gun-belt mentality, but George truly saw people as lost and was loving them in their lostness. It was profound to me. And for me to see this everyday, that it wasn't an act, but rather that it was a true pious zealousness."

In those 10 years of ministry in Crawfordsville, the Lord birthed not only a church through George and Pam Markey, but also outreaches that would affect people and churches across the community and beyond. Through George's invitation and leadership, both Nicky Cruz and Franklin Graham came and held crusades in the area. The focus was on reaching those who were in darkness and uniting the churches through a passion for evangelism. In truth, there seem to be so many matters that divide churches, but it seems that the one issue that has the potential of developing unity is when churches work together to share the message of salvation with those who do not know Jesus.

LABORERS FOR THE HARVEST

With a heart for missions, George frequently had missionaries share at church. The ultimate goal was that people would see the need of reaching out not only to the local community, but to the ends of the earth. It does seem to be a truth that unless the pastor has a vision for missions, the church will not be much of a missionary-sending or -supporting church. Mike Abney recalls, "There were times when over half of the church budget went to missions. George did not take a salary for a long time, but kept working with his hands and gave so that the church could support more missionaries." This example of a passion for the lost and the world did not go by unnoticed.

The time came when David Wray made plans to attend Bible College in southern California. "George was the first one to support me financially when I went to Bible school. Then when I felt a call to Mexico, I called him and George said, 'Go and we'll support you,' and he gave me $300 a month to live on when I was down there. He was a tremendous influence for me when I went to Mexico."

A BODY REACHING UP

A passionate commitment to the coming Kingdom of God compels us to minister to each other, as well as to those who do not yet have this hope of heaven. It is discouraging and even dangerous if this part of the vision is sidelined and not kept in front of the people. George often said, "People don't sing about heaven anymore." In fact, he frequently reminisced about the early days of growing up in the Lord, standing around a piano and singing songs about heaven. Himself affected early on by the death of his mother, and having studied from the prophets to the Book of Revelation, George was fully convinced in his heart of the realities of heaven and the future awaiting us as believers. "If you were raised with Christ, seek those things which are above, where Christ is, sitting at the right hand of God" (Col. 3:1).

Perhaps for this very reason, George was the most heavenly minded person I have ever met. I have heard it said that "a person can be so heavenly minded that they are no earthly good." However, in actuality I don't think a person can be any earthly good if they are not heavenly minded. A right perspective of eternity guides one's life, affections, and actions while here on this earth. George constantly reminded those around him that Jesus is the center not only of this life, but also of a glorious life to come. Furthermore, an expectancy of heaven makes the pains of this life more bearable. Whether bound by the pain in life, the death of a loved one, or the burdens of the daily grind, heaven unshackles us from the grips of this world and centers our affections on the place for which God created us.

LONGING FOR HEAVEN, WAITING IN WORSHIP

If I had to describe George's theology in one word, it would be heaven. George longed for heaven, and desired for those around him to be instilled with a passion for eternity. Worship for George was simply a preparation for what those of us who know Jesus will experience in heaven. Observing George as he worshiped was contagious—it made you want to enter into the Holy of Holies right at that moment. With arms stretched out, eyes toward heaven, smile on his face, and sometimes tears rolling down his cheeks, George would stand in worship on the front row in church as if he were in the very throne room of God. Tom Camp was the worship leader and remembers, "George was the biggest worshiper. He was always on the front row and his voice was so loud that I could hear it over the monitors." In reality, George was the worship leader even though he was not on the stage. In fact, George disagreed with the modern teaching on worship that a worship leader needs to be invisible. It's true, a person should not be a distraction, and there are many who stand up in front of the people who are more of a distraction, but a worship leader needs to be just that—a leader of the people into worship. Someone who will guide you into the presence of God. I have never heard a pastor say that a pastor should be invisible, but I have heard pastors say that about worship leaders. One thing is certain: A worship leader whose life is not visibly full of worship, on and off the stage, will not be able to properly lead the people in worship.

END TIMES

Himself longing for the rapture of the Church, George was intent on understanding what the Bible had to say about the last days. Not for the purpose of instilling fear into the people, as so many preachers and churches do today, but rather to learn these truths for the purpose of showing people the glorious future that awaited them as children of God. I clearly remember sitting with George one evening, Bibles open to the book of I Thessalonians. I was asking question after question of George, seeking to understand the rapture, the resurrection of the righteous, and our eternal bodies. Never being one to give an answer that he didn't know when he could not determine the meaning of a certain passage, George said, "Well, let's call pastor Chuck." He immediately grabbed the phone, got through to pastor Chuck Smith, and asked him the questions that were troubling us. I walked away that day with a clearer picture of heaven than I ever had before, and an understanding that this hope was now my favorite theme of Scripture as well.

A pastor who does not have an adequate theology of heaven is often a pastor who is motivating people through fear, works, and the law. We have two choices, just as Peter did that day on the Sea of Galilee. We can walk by fear, seeing the waves surrounding us, or we can walk by faith with eyes fixed on Jesus and the hope that we will soon be with Him. It is this hope of heaven that is an anchor for our souls. It is this hope of heaven that saves us. It is the hope of heaven that drives us to the point where we long to escape this sinful body and its desires so we can experience that fullness of the presence of God. But rather than giving us an escapist mentality, as some critics accuse, this hope further roots our feet in this life so that we can comfort those who are going through trials and sufferings and so that we can take as many people with us to heaven as possible. We know where our true citizenship lies, in heaven, and we want to be good ambassadors while we are here on this earth. We have no fanciful conjectures that the Kingdom of God will be established by man on this earth, but rather that the Kingdom of God will come in power only when the perfect Son of God comes in glory.

George frequently quoted the words the Apostle Paul used when he wrote to the Philippians, "For me to live is Christ, to die is gain" (Phil. 1:21). I think Paul's desire reflects the heart of a person touched by heaven. "For I am hard-pressed between the two, having a desire to depart and be with Christ, which is far better. Nevertheless to remain in the flesh is more needful for you." (Phil. 1:23-24) Can it be said of the Apostle Paul that he was so heavenly minded that he was no earthly good? Of course not! As the farmer plowing the field must look afar off, keeping his destination in sight so as to plow in a straight line, so the Christian must keep his focus on that glorious, eternal promise awaiting him, so as not to be skewed in task or sidetracked in purpose.

KEEPING A LIGHT TOUCH ON THIS WORLD

One of the plagues of the American church is hypocrisy, that woeful trait in which one's life does not measure up to one's words. What would it be like to preach about the need to "Go into all the world and preach the Gospel" if one did not have a heart for missions? What would it be like if someone preached about the need to be generous, but rarely gave of his own his time or resources? And what would it be like if a person preached about heaven, but his lifestyle reflected more of a concern with being satisfied in this world?

George not only preached about heaven but lived for it. His earthly home was remarkably simple, his cars frequently lacking in repair, his hard-earned money frequently given away. For example, every winter George would wrap half of the farmhouse in plastic so that it would be warm enough for his family. Tom Camp shares, "He could have had more, but he always wanted to do more for the people." Gayle Erwin remembers staying in George and Pam's home. He says, "Their home was adequate, but was not fancifully furnished. The table and chairs might not be matching, but they were happy."

The family continued to grow in size as Jonathan, number seven, was born in February of 1986. With such great needs at home, some believed that George was not directing enough resources toward his family. Mike Abney shares, "The biggest rebuke I ever got from George was one time when I saw him give away his entire paycheck. I told him 'George, we worked hard, and you've got kids.' George looked at me sternly and said, 'Mike, God sees to my needs!' And God did. His kids didn't go without." Mike continues, "He gave his money to other families. There was one family that the church supported for an entire year, and there is just now fruit coming from that. He was always giving, never expecting anything in return." For George, the verse in Hebrews was lived out in his life: "For here we have no continuing city, but we seek the one to come" (Heb. 13:14). His was a life and vision guided by heaven.

14

THE VISION REJECTED

PAIN. That's the word that David Wray uses in describing George during this time. "Just tremendous amounts of pain. Pain as a young pastor before Crawfordsville and then during Crawfordsville. Pain, disappointment, betrayal. He went through a lot of pain, and as a result he experienced an intimacy with God and a greater strength from the Scriptures. He learned that if God could bring him comfort through the Word while enduring pain in his life, God would do that in the lives of other people."

As the church in Crawfordsville grew, George's vision expanded with it. His heart was to begin a Christian school, and he did. His desire was to get a piece of property for the construction of a new church facility, and he did. George found a piece of property not far from where the church was meeting. It was in a wooded area, up on the top of a hill. "The church was growing like crazy," remembers Mike Abney. "When we looked at the property, George, Chuck Smith, and myself went up there. We looked and prayed, and it seemed like God was saying, 'This is it; go for it.'" A no-interest loan was obtained, the property was purchased, and the clearing of the land began. Mike continues, "We worked up there every week, clearing weeds, cutting trees. That is when the hearts of men began emerging."

As George continued to lead in the vision that he believed God had given to him, resistance to both George and his vision began to appear among certain individuals in the church. Some of those who home-schooled their children came out against the idea of a school. Some of the leaders in the church began resisting the idea of a building. It seemed that the greater the vision, the greater the resistance to its implementation. If the following hasn't been said, it probably should: If one wants to see division within a church, just start a building program. Mike shares, "George had a vision when no one else did. It frustrated him. I remember being on the roof with him working, and his mind was on the church the whole time. When you have a vision, you want to move. You can't sit still. But the elders didn't trust him, because they saw his failings as a man." You cannot separate the vision from the man, any more than you can separate the prophecy from the prophet. God can and does use many people for His purposes, but that is just it—He uses people, men with feet of clay who are by no means perfect.

Meeting after meeting was called in attempts to figure out what the real issues were. Mike remembers, "When the split started, we had several meetings trying to get people together and find out what was going on. George allowed the men to express themselves and what they thought. It turned out, though, that many of the men had a problem with me, that a man who had an alcohol problem in the past and that someone who could not read and write was allowed to be an elder. I said, 'George, this is because of me.' George answered, saying, 'Mike, it isn't because of you. It's because of the hardness of their hearts.' That's what came out from those meetings." Remarkably, another issue that came to the surface was that some of the men took issue with George for so publicly voicing his opinion about the KKK when he stood in protest against their racist march.

Complaint after complaint was levied against George. I remember George saying that for years he used to carry around an index card with a list of complaints that the elders had given to him. One complaint I recall him sharing was their feeling that he did not trust them. The example given involved the purchase of a lawnmower. George had asked one of the elders to buy a lawnmower, but at the last minute had called and asked whether he could accompany the man who was to buy it. This was the example given to George that he did not trust the leadership around him, since George apparently felt that he had to go and make the decision about the lawnmower himself. George's explanation to the man? "I just wanted to be with you, because I have a good time when I am with you."

During a congregational meeting on April 23, 1989, the church body was informed by the elders that any financial support for George would be cut off in June. In this moment of discouragement, Tom Camp remembers George telling him, "Sometimes the loneliest place in the world is to be a pastor. There are some things that pastors go through that the people will never know." Tom shares, "I tried to argue with George when he said that, but now as a pastor I believe it."

David Wray recalls returning home to Crawfordsville from Mexico for a short furlough. He shares, "The wife of one of the leaders ran into me at a Kroger's and gave me a bunch of Old Testament references saying that if I don't get out, I was going to go down in flames." Pam Markey recalls certain "prophecies" spoken against them saying that she and George would be divorced, that their children would turn against them and God, and basically that their lives would be ruined. Whether entire families, or women who had been trusted friends, or co-leaders and teachers, many began to grow hostile at worst, or indifferent at best, to George and Pam.

George was difficult to console and encourage, especially in times like these. In fact, it seemed that the only encouragement he would receive was that which came from the Lord. During this difficult season, Pam also seemed to find consolation only in the Lord. She recorded in her journal an entry about Moses and the bitter waters of Marah. "I have indeed come to a place of bitter waters, but we came here by Your command. Let the cross take the bitterness out and turn the waters sweet that we may flourish and grow."

When the time came for a congregational vote for the removal of George as pastor, Amy Repasky was doing secretarial work at the church. Amy shares, "George never said one word bad about anyone during that time. In fact, I had no clue what was going on. I was at Maranatha [the name of the Christian School started at the church] one day, and George was in the office on the phone. I overheard him and I could tell by the conversation what was going on. I ran down to Pam and told her that I really wasn't snooping, but that I could not help hearing, that I had heard about the split. I went home and found Calvary Chapel of Costa Mesa's telephone number. I talked with a secretary there and just said, 'Would you please have Chuck Smith call me? I am with Calvary Chapel of Crawfordsville.' I didn't say anything else and didn't know if he would ever call me back, but he did.

He just said that he would work something out, and then he made plans to come in a couple of weeks."

Even when George was asked to step down, his heart was for the people going through this difficult time. Tom Camp recalls, "We couldn't find a pastor, and the elders were doing the speaking. George kept saying that they need to find a pastor. He said, 'You have to start shepherding His people.'" Eventually the church of upwards of 500 people dwindled down to about 30. Tom Camp remembers, "When Chuck Smith flew in, I think there were three elders left at the time. Pastor Chuck asked about the symptoms of what George was doing: 'What was the sin? Was there immorality or stealing involved?' The elders answered that there was no open sin; they just felt that stress had gotten to George.'" On May 28, 1989, Pastor Chuck mediated the congregational vote, and George won by about six votes. After inquiring of George whether he wanted to stay, Pastor Chuck announced that since George was not voted out as pastor, the elders had to leave.

"Before the division I remember going out and seeing that property," remembers David Wray. "It was a big dream. A dream in George's heart that was killed. I learned that church splits don't happen. The term 'split' gives you the idea that people go to different sides, but most of those people just fell through the middle. Many of those people remained unchurched for years. They didn't split into another church; they just fell through the cracks. I don't blame George or anybody for that, but that's just a strange thing to say when something like that happens, that a church splits. In reality, people just get lost in the shuffle."

Reading through Pam's journals from 1989 gives one a taste of the torment, trials, and tragedy that occurred. Pam writes out of a mixture of both frustration and faith. It seems that through this time her spiritual insights into the Word grew much deeper, more intense, and very intimate, perhaps also the result of her suffering. In one entry from June 2 Pam writes, 'All those who stood with us are gone away, all those whose hands were supportive and dedicated to working together are gone away. My heart fails within me. Is this to be yet another chapter of pain and suffering? Oh, God, we are at Your mercy. Father, purify my heart before you that I would not hold bitterness or anger. Build George up to be the man that you would have him to be – You have allowed him to be torn down, now build him up by the power of Your Spirit." In another place she reveals the rawness of her soul and her personal struggle to trust anyone again as she writes, "I feel naked under a buttonless coat that I must clutch about me carefully – to forget is to be exposed, vulnerable, and shamed."

WHY?

Some have suggested that George's own openness about his flesh and his weaknesses was repulsive to certain individuals. Whether when he preached about working with sheep and watching them defecate in their own troughs, or when he shared of his own struggles with rage – the result on one occasion being his wrapping of a defective lawnmower around a tree – it seemed that some people preferred a perfect pastor, one free from flesh and vice but filled with only virtue and victory. Better to put on an air of perfection and give people a lofty goal to strive for, than for them to see imperfections and our need to reply on God's perfect, saving, and empowering grace.

Others have noted George's apparent lack of tact in dealing with difficult people. When it became apparent that a prominent member of the church was involved in improper business dealings, George's reaction was to confront the evil and warn others of the "wolf." In no uncertain words he expressed his righteous indignation about such a man to the leadership, but the resulting gasps of certain women and expressions of horror were in the direction of George rather than the wolf. George was not one to do anything out of obligation, or because someone gave money, or to save face. It seemed to them to matter more how he talked to someone than whether he was telling them the truth. He wasn't a people-pleaser.

Still others have noted the differences in the church government and philosophy of ministry between George and those in this traditional Midwestern community. Brian Hudson shares, "The Calvary Chapel understanding of polity and church government is the Moses model. Moses is the head, then there are elders who support the head, but unless something outrageous happens their purpose is not to remove a pastor. The pastor has been called by God and people come along to support him and his vision. However, [one of the elders] believed that church government should be collegial, ruled by elders of which the pastor was the visionary leader but an equal to the elders. Really, I think the church split happened over a difference of philosophy that had never been articulated. When [this certain elder] wanted George to submit to the elders, George had no clue. To him, that's not how you do church. And [this elder] had a different philosophy. It all kept escalating until it fell apart, but if they would have dealt with that issue – that there exists more than one form of church government, but we are a Calvary and if you don't like that you probably need to step down or go somewhere else if that is not your understanding of church government – it would have been better."

But, instead, these people were embittered and kept coming. They would pass notes during the services, or forbid their children to speak with George and Pam's children. They masked their contempt of George and his ability to be an example by leveling a plethora of accusations at him, such as saying that he did not spend enough time with his family. Diana Faulk comments, "I am loyal by personality, so I did not want to be blind to what was happening. I sought the Lord, and the result was that I decided to follow the fruit. I just knew George's heart. So for me it became clear that 'as for me and my house we are going to serve the Lord.'" However, it seems that most people did not want to be forced into choosing sides. They thought that by leaving, they would escape the conflict. But in reality, their departure merely gave greater voice to the embittered people who decided to stay for their own ambitions, personal gain, or self-seeking.

THE RESULT

The result of the "split" was the formation of another church, which itself fractured several more times, and whose leaders ended up turning on one another and devouring each other. My own experience has been that if a church is begun by embittered people and built on division, their own bitterness and divisiveness will soon lead to the eventual decline and decimation of the church.

Mike Abney shares, "George told me, 'Try your best to know the hearts of your men,' and the hearts of these men weren't right. They would say one thing, but in their hearts was something else. I remember that George would walk out the door after a board meeting, and these men would turn to me and start saying, 'Mike, we really don't need to build.' I got confused. These other men, I was in their lives so much. But the ways that these men would flatter me or George. There was one time when me and George went to

Kentucky. On the way down George was reading in the Bible about flattery. He told me, 'Mike, if someone flatters you, they don't like you.'"

Though George was enduring apparent abandonment, behind-the-back comments, flat-out lies, and betrayal, what seemed to hurt him the most was not even really about him. Mike and Tom both recount the following story, almost word for word. Mike recalls, "Tom and I were driving with George in the van one day, and all of a sudden George was crying so hard. He was holding his chest. I thought he was having a heart attack. He pulled off the road and his body collapsed into the steering wheel, heaving. We put our arms around him and tried to pray, and he said, 'If only they knew, if only they knew what they were doing to their children.' Over and over he said that. That's what he thought about, their little children and how they were destroying their children and the growth of the church."

Years later, after George's passing, in a letter sent to Pam and the family from one of those involved in the division, a man writes, "Here is where I went wrong and where so many others went wrong. The need to be right became the most important thing. When that happens, the ability to 'be like Christ' comes to an end. One can be right and not be like Christ. If this was a test, I failed it miserably. You were a victim of my failure and for that I am truly sorry. I know I was not alone, but I am not concerned about others who may have failed, I am concerned about my failure and my relationship with you. I was blind at the time. The children of the Calvary Chapel families were the innocent victims of our mishandling of the situation. God in His grace has faithfully navigated most of those children through the spiritual collateral damage of that event, but I am concerned that there are a number who may not have fared so well."

KADESH BARNEA

Kadesh Barnea was a recurring theme in many of George's messages and conversations both during and after the time of the church division. As the children of Israel approached the Promised Land, 12 spies were chosen by Moses to go in and scope out the fruitfulness of the land, the cities, and the peoples. Upon returning, 10 of the 12 spies gave reports of a luscious and plenteous land. Nevertheless, they also shared of the impossibilities in taking it, that the enemies of Israel were there – the Amalekites, Jebusites, Amorites, and Canaanites. Not only that, but there were giants in the land,

and the spies were as grasshoppers to them. Who in their right mind would think that they could conquer this land?

Only two of the spies, Joshua and Caleb, took the Lord at His Word and trusted Him for great things. They said, "Let us go up at once and take possession, for we are well able to overcome it." (Numbers 13:30) They warned the people not to rebel against the Lord, yet the people prepared to stone them. The 10 unfaithful spies caused the hearts of the people to melt with fear. It was as if they were saying, "Don't remind us of the previous promises and the victories, for they are but tied to our weakness and sin. We know of what we are capable, what is best for our families." Oh how quickly man tends to forget his own sin and tendency toward rebellion.

A couple chapters before this account in the Book of Numbers, we read of the complaining and grumbling of the people, which is soon followed by the dissension of Aaron and Miriam, Moses' own family. Furthermore, after God's chiding for their unbelief, we read of the defeat of Israel as they decided to go up in their own strength. Yet we read that Caleb had a different spirit in him and had followed the Lord fully.

What could have taken only 11 days ended up taking 40 years because of unbelief, lack of faith, a refusal to go forward. The vision was rejected, the logic of man was elevated, the fears of man were heeded. How can a leader continue to lead if the people do not support the vision? The outcome of that congregational vote, and the preceding months of rebellion, was that certain people did not have faith to go forward, and virtually all of that generation died in the wilderness as a result.

What is the place of Kadesh Barnea in our lives? George believed that there are many times in our lives when the Lord wants to take us into a place of blessing, of fruitfulness. He brings us to a place of decision, perhaps even giving us a glimpse of that which He wants to do. Yes, there will be battles, there will be dissenting voices, and there will be open rebellion, whether in our own hearts or the hearts of those around us. But the decision always remains before us at those times – will we take God at His Word, trust in His leading, provision, and strength, or will we operate in the flesh? Better to follow a vision founded on faith than to flounder in a morass of mediocrity, placating the fleshliness of the multitudes.

As George and Pam remained serving the wounded church, soon people began returning—new people began coming. Pam shares, "George believed that if the congregational vote resulted in our favor that we should stay. We had been given a verse from the Book Revelation saying 'strengthen that which remains.' And so we stayed and ministered to the body. The truth is, the Lord ministered to us through this wonderful body of people as well."

THE WRECK

September 19, 1991 – The article in the Crawfordsville Journal Review begins, "An accident this morning involving a van and a semi-tractor trailer sent nine people to Culver Union Hospital, according to a Montgomery County police officer." George and Mike Abney were working together on a roof when news of the accident reached them. Minutes later they arrived at the tragic, but strangely peaceful, scene. With his bleeding and injured family lying strewn over a farmer's field, George tenderly approached each one to assess the situation. Renee, who had been driving the van, was the only person who was not injured, and she spent her time going to each person, praying with them, and making them as comfortable as possible until the arrival of the ambulances. One officer who arrived at the scene was shocked at the lack of hysteria and chaos. After the initial collision, pain, and emotional outbursts, prayer brought the peace of God into the middle of the situation.

Broken legs, broken arms, concussions, lacerations, and other physical traumas were the result of this accident. Pam, who was pregnant with Aaron, their eighth child, had suffered a concussion. She was bandaged up and would later be released from the hospital with the assurance that everything was normal with the baby. Robin, however, was listed in critical condition and life-lined by helicopter to Methodist Hospital in Indianapolis. Her pulse was lost twice during the flight to the hospital. As she lay in a coma in intensive care, it was unknown what would happen to her. If she did wake up, no one knew what the extent of the brain injuries she had sustained would be.

I remember going to the hospital in Indianapolis to visit Robin, and seeing the gut-wrenching, pain-mixed-with-love expression on George's face as he sought to communicate to his once jovial and energetic but now vacant and emotionless daughter. That evening as George raced back to Crawfordsville to care for the rest of the family, Vi Goodrich, wife of Bill Goodrich, pastor of Horizon Christian Fellowship in Indianapolis, spent the first night in the hospital with Robin. The next morning, Pam managed to get herself quickly released from the Crawfordsville hospital. Eager to see Robin, George and Pam left for Indianapolis. Arriving at the hospital, Pam rushed to Robin's side. Vi shares, "I remember Pam leaning over Robin, her tears falling on Robin's face as the nurse listed all the details of Robin's grave and unresponsive condition. And then, all of a sudden, George leaned over and called out in that wonderful deep voice of his the most beautiful words I've ever heard and that I will never forget: 'ROBIN! ROBIN! IT'S DADDY!' And immediately Robin's eyes popped open, staring straight up into space! She heard her daddy's voice! And that marked a turnaround, a hope, the beginning of Robin's long healing process." Vi continues, "Engraved in my heart forever are those four beautiful words from a loving father's heart to his child. In George, I saw the heart of my Father God, 'My sheep hear My voice, and I know them and they follow Me'" (John 10:27).

After a few days, Robin finally did wake up for good, but it was obvious that she had been severely affected by the accident. Not sure of who she was, Robin was speaking incoherently. She had short-term memory loss, partial paralysis on the left side, and a lack of any kind of emotion, and she was in need of being physically restrained so that she would not injure herself. As the days turned into weeks and Robin began walking again, even strolls down the hall proved to be strenuous. Whenever they drew near to an elevator, Robin would begin leaning in that direction, wanting to leave the hospital. At one point she concluded that the quickest way to exit the hospital would be by jumping out of the window. Pam spent almost all of this time by her side in the hospital. At one point in her journal Pam writes, "Robin got up and I asked her what she was doing, and she said, 'Just let me die.'" As the doctors continued their testing, observation, and occupational therapy, things began to look up. Pam was informed that it would take Robin months to fully recover, but that she should be able to go home in only a few weeks. As she began to improve, music became the language of comfort and restoration during this time as Robin filled the halls with songs played on a piano in the hospital. When she did get home, the first thing she did was to kiss the floor, and then play the piano.

Not once does Renee recall being chastised or lectured about the accident. Parents frequently use such tragedies as "teaching tools," or times to lecture, and even take out their frustrations on their children. Renee remembers that it was never an issue. In fact, the family was concerned that Renee would be overly distraught over the accident, beating herself up over what could not be changed. God would teach anything that needed to be taught, and the main lessons had already been learned. The family's job was to show forgiveness, love, and support.

People in the church and community flooded George and his family with support. Whether by making meals, taking trips to the hospitals to visit and care for the needs of the family, or helping take care of the children and things around the house, many of those who had grown so close to the Markeys over the previous decade came together as the body of Christ to show love and support at a time of great need. Even the Wendy's restaurant in Crawfordsville sent flowers to the family while they were in the hospital. Multitudes of people who had gone through the church division began contacting George, showering him with support, love, and encouragement. However, what could have been a time for the renewal of cold hearts affected by the earlier church division turned out to be a further hardening of hearts for some. Mike Abney remembers, "When the family got in the wreck, it was everybody's chance to renew and restore relationship with the Markeys, but still there were those who were not happy with George. What person's heart isn't going to go out to a family who has endured this tragedy? This is your chance. But they hardened their hearts even more. I think God simply said, 'OK, I am taking this blessing out of town.' The blessing went to Ukraine."

SECTION 2 PHOTOS

George's first trip to Israel with Calvary Chapel of Costa Mesa, 1977.

George officiating the wedding of Alan and LaRhonda Zachary, June 1981.

A baptism during a church conference at Camp Talitha, September 1981.

George in the early 1980s.

An amazing couple, George and Pam, June 1981.

Taking the young church to the Pennsylvania conference,
with Chuck Smith and Raul Ries.

Having fun at a church celebration, October 1987.

George in his "office" at Wendy's.

The Markeys in 1987. Back Row: Pam, Robin, George Robert, Renee, George.
Front Row: Jonathan, Melanie, Rhonda, David.

Pastor Dave Keesee, Mike Abney, and George at Mike and Lyn Abney's Wedding.

SECTION 3

THE DEPARTURE OF THE MAN

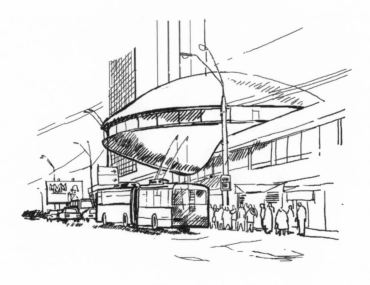

CHAPTER FIFTEEN

NEW BEGINNINGS

IN THE MONTHS preceding the accident, the Lord had been working in various ways to prepare George and his family for a new season of life and ministry. Unsettledness gripped the hearts of George and Pam. Writing in her journal, Pam acknowledges the fact that she was "constantly feeling out of harmony with those around me." A little later she records, "In many ways, we don't seem to be significantly better off than we were before. There are sparks here and there, hopeful signs, but then we are so fragmented and at odds." The rebuilding of those lives that had been torn apart by the recent division would take much time to accomplish. In truth, a trust that has been broken in moments can take years to mend, if it mends at all. Forgiveness and the restoration of trust are two separate issues, and it was crucial not only that forgiveness take place, but that trust be restored for true fellowship to begin again.

It was during this time of struggle and restoration that the Lord brought new life from the cold ashes of division, and the seeds of that new life came from a relationship that had begun even before Calvary Chapel. Years earlier, Dave Keesee and George Markey had met at a fish fry in New Ross, Indiana, at the time when George was pastoring the church there. Having gotten saved while playing in a rock band, Dave began changing all of the lyrics of their songs to ones with a Christian message. With a passion for the Word of God and a gift for teaching, Dave became involved in a new church that was beginning in Crawfordsville, one that seemed fresh and alive and was soon attracting many people. However, a struggle soon began in Dave's heart. It was a struggle that was coming from two men whom he loved. His own pastor and George Markey were two pastors whom he greatly respected, but they held differing views on many important biblical matters. When Calvary Chapel began in Crawfordsville, Dave began noticing a difference between the people in his church and those attending Calvary Chapel. "I taught a home Bible study, and there were people coming from the church that I was attending as well as from George's church. Those in Calvary knew the Word of God; they knew the books of the Bible. I would say, 'Turn to the book of Zechariah,' and while the people from my church were flipping through the New Testament trying to find the book of Zechariah, the people from George's church were immediately turning to the book in the Old Testament." Those in Calvary seemed joyful in spite of life's difficulties. Those in Dave's church were placing a great emphasis on victorious faith, emotional experience, and financial freedom. It was, as Chuck Smith so aptly phrased it, "charisma versus charismania." The biggest issue, however, came down to a discrepancy in teachings concerning the doctrine of the sovereignty of God, and it was then that Dave realized that he could not merge the two teachings. Painfully, but with a longing for the pure Word of God, Dave and his family decided to leave the church where they had been serving and move to Calvary Chapel.

Sitting under George's teaching, Dave continued to increase in his love for the Word of God. Both Dave and his wife, Angie, became a part of the life of the growing church. However, after a period of time, Dave was asked by people in the neighboring town of North Salem to come and begin teaching at a small church there. After several months of Dave traveling there by himself to minister, the family finally moved and began pastoring that congregation. Like George, Dave worked in carpentry at the same time that he was pastoring. Dave shares, "George was very gracious and very generous. He gave me fifty dollars a week so that I could take one afternoon off a week to study. And he supported me like that for at least a year."

It was during this time when Dave was pastoring in North Salem that the division in the church in Crawfordsville occurred. Although hearing about what was happening from a distance, and saddened by it, Dave was left untainted by any of the groups who were fracturing into various camps.

The division in Calvary Chapel of Crawfordsville was a tragedy that was observed from a distance.

Soon after the division, Dave found himself returning to the Crawfordsville area, ministering to those people from his congregation in North Salem who had moved there. Dave shares, "When we moved back, it didn't make sense to start another church since there was already a good, Bible-teaching church [Calvary Chapel] there. We were doing the same thing, and we were in the area together." Dave and George talked and decided that they would merge the two churches. Dave and his group would begin attending Calvary, and Dave and George would both co-pastor the congregation. Dave continues, "George was so gracious. He just always believed in me. And he gave me the pulpit for a year. Only later on did it become clear, as George and I would talk, that he felt that he was to be moving on."

With an unsettledness in their hearts, and now an able and like-minded pastor serving beside George, George and Pam were open to new direction from the Lord. Interestingly, Pam has recorded in her journal from November 12, 1991, a prayer for Russia. Even earlier, in 1988, she has recorded that George was reading the book Revolution in World Missions. Other journal and calendar notes and entries highlight the peoples of the Soviet Union, one even mentioning the Kyrgyz people.

In January of 1992, Pam gave birth to Aaron, their eighth and last biological child. In the Scriptures, the number eight is symbolic of a time of new beginnings. George and Pam felt that perhaps the Lord was showing them, even through this child, that there would soon be a season of fresh, new beginnings in their lives and ministry.

NEW DIRECTION

It was at Horizon Christian fellowship in Indianapolis that George received new direction. On the last day of a weeklong inductive Bible study training course for pastors, Dan Finfrock ended the session by showing the pastors a video by Bill Bright, vividly detailing the new openness to the Gospel in Russia. Just a few short months earlier the Iron Curtain of communism had finally been stripped away, revealing its millions of spiritually starved people.

For decades, believers around the world had been praying for the people of the Soviet Union, for a way through the veil of spiritual lies and deceit. The people had been indoctrinated, believing that Christians were backward-thinking, deluded, and even dangerous. Rumors had been circulated that Christians were killing children, eating their flesh, and drinking their blood in ritualistic ceremonies. Students had been kept from higher education simply because of their Christian faith. Children had been forcibly separated from believing parents. Untold numbers of people had been imprisoned, or exiled to the harsh, frozen wastelands of Siberia, or even brutally executed for believing that Jesus is Lord, and not Lenin, the founder of the Soviet Empire. For years, Bibles had to be secretly smuggled into the Soviet Union from the West. Now that the wall had fallen, the Gospel could go in freely to these newly independent nations.

Recalling that day at Horizon, Pastor Dave Keesee shares, "Dan Finfrock finished the session by saying, 'I would like to show you a film about Russia, and what is going on there.' When George saw that video, you could see the lights come on in his mind, and he turned to me thinking that I would be just as excited about it as he was. But I said, 'George, it's Russia.' After this video, he immediately began looking for a quick way over there." Finding a group of Calvary Chapel pastors who would be traveling to Russia in May, George signed up.

That trip would take George to Moscow, St. Petersburg, and Kiev, the three largest cities of the former Soviet Union. However, it was not until he arrived in Kiev, Ukraine, that George sensed God wanted to use him to minister to the people in this specific place. His calling was confirmed by an invitation from one of the local Protestant churches to come and pastor their congregation, as well as an invitation from the group The Victims of the Chernobyl Disaster. Excited by this sense of calling and confirmation, George made the long-distance phone call home to speak with Pam and the kids. Renee remembers the family gathering on her parents' bed upstairs where the phone was located. She shares, "Dad called and asked, 'How would you like to live in Kiev?' It was a very exciting time for the family."

BAND OF BROTHERS

Upon his return from Russia and Ukraine, George began sharing with the pastors in the Midwest. Pastor Bill Goodrich remembers speaking with

George. "When he got back, George told me, 'Bill, I think I'm supposed to go to Ukraine.' I said, 'OK, that's nice, George.' And he said, 'Bill, you don't understand. I think we are going to move to Ukraine.' I asked him when, and he replied that it would probably be early that summer. George was set in stone." Upon seeing Bill's questioning response, George added, "Why wouldn't I go? There is a need. No one is teaching. There is a need. I feel God has spoken to me." Bill continues, "My part in all of it then became just to walk through it with him and encourage him, and then he would be gone."

It was back in 1986 when Bill had first met George. "I am going to introduce you to a man with no guile," Pastor Joe Bell said to Bill Goodrich as they were driving out to George's farm. "You mean like Nathaniel?" Bill inquired. "Yes, like Nathaniel, in the Bible," Joe responded. Having come from San Diego, California, to start a church in Indianapolis, Bill Goodrich immediately began looking for people with whom he could fellowship, other pastors with whom he could pray and be accountable. Joe Bell, serving in Lafayette, was the first pastor Bill contacted, and Joe told Bill that he needed to meet this man, George Markey. "The directions to George's house were unlike any I had ever heard before," remarks Bill. "'Go down this road about five miles. Turn left at this big rock. Continue straight, go over a gulley...' When I finally got there, I thought that I was out in the middle of nowhere." The relationship that formed between Bill and George in those last few years before his departure to Ukraine was unlike any other relationship Bill had experienced. "If you knew George, you knew George. There were no ulterior motives, no deception in any way. He had a pure heart," shares Bill. In the beginning of the ministry in Indianapolis, Bill encountered many difficulties. "There were issues of sin with a leader of another church there in Indianapolis. I would meet with George and Joe to pray through things together. George would say, 'Keep going, Bill.' He was a real friend. George and Joe were on the board of our church to provide accountability for me." Now, this group of pastors was sending out one of their own. A man who had been a pioneer in the Midwest was being sent out to begin churches in the former Soviet country of Ukraine.

George believed that a missionary should never go to the foreign field without being sent by and held accountable to a church or group of churches. For him it was crucial that he have the support of those pastors and churches he knew and respected. Soon, Joe Bell, Bill Goodrich, Dave Keesee, Ed Gaines, Gary Rifenburg, and other pastors from the Midwest came together to pray over George regarding this new direction for him and his family. The collective message to him was, 'You go, and we will support you.' Calvary Chapel of Costa Mesa even sent funds to cover the cost of the plane tickets for the entire family. The date for the departure was set for July 3, 1992, less than six weeks away.

THE COUNTDOWN

Regarding her thoughts about George's plan to leave in such a short time, Pam, already a well-seasoned traveler, shares, "I didn't say anything to George, but I thought, 'He is so naive,' because in my mind I thought, 'There is no way that you can pack up ten people, get all of those passports and visas, and move to another country in just over a month.' So I thought, 'Lord, you tell him.'" But that which seemed illogical in the minds of many, including Pam, turned out to be the plan of God. As George was set in his decision, believing that the Lord wanted to use them in Ukraine at this opportune time, the Lord went before them in all of their preparations for the move. With only a month and a half remaining until their scheduled departure, George and Pam had to not only pack up an entire family, but get the necessary passports and visas as well. This task was further complicated by the fact that David's birth at home had not been planned and his birth certificate had not been obtained until after Jonathan was born nearly two years later. As a result, the U.S. government required many extra documents and proofs before they would even grant David a one-year passport. During this short time, long road trips to Indianapolis and Chicago became a common occurrence to obtain all of the documents necessary for travel.

Although Pam and most of the kids were excited about the opportunity to live and serve the Lord on the foreign mission field, two of the children were reluctant in the beginning. "Little George" was no longer little. Now 16 years of age and sporting a driver's license, George Robert was just coming of age and had interest in a girl from church. Robin was turning 14, and also was hesitant to leave. Wisely, George asked them to pray about it and said that it would be a one-year commitment. Before they left, each of his children had come up to him and shared that they were in favor of going. George Robert agreed that he could put his life and ambitions on hold. After all, it would be only for a year. Melanie shares, "It didn't feel temporary. Even though Dad said that we were going for 'a year,' we were getting rid of everything. We were finding people to live in the house. To me it felt like it was going to be long-term."

Even though the family was united in looking forward to their upcoming departure, not everyone around them was as elated. Many people questioned George as he was preparing to lead his large family into an unstable, unknown, and perhaps even dangerous environment. The questions filled their ears: "You don't know where you are going to live? You don't know the language? How is this going to affect the future of your children? How are they going to be educated? Don't you think that there are enough needs here? Everyone has seen the 'bread lines' on television – how could you take your family there?" But perhaps the most difficult charges to bear were the onslaughts and accusations that were spoken to George by other pastors and leaders. In fact, the man who led George's first trip to Russia and Ukraine was dogmatic in saying that George should not go. His thinking was that a family on the mission field would do more harm than good, that all of their time would be focused on the family and there would be little time for any kind of real ministry. As the questioning seeped into their hearts and the accusations rang out, Pam began to fear that their large family might disqualify them from going. "I began to wonder if my ambitions for being a missionary were overcoming the reality in which I was living," shares Pam. "I began to think, 'Perhaps it is better that only single people or couples with no children go to the field.'" Amidst all of the commotion, Pam's father, John, actually spoke what would become a word of prophecy for them. "My dad told me, 'What people think will be your greatest detriment will actually turn out to be your greatest asset.' After that I quit worrying about all of the other voices. I remembered the call and I followed my husband."

On June 6, 1992, the article in the Journal Review began with the following: "They'll miss their friends and some conveniences, but George and Pam Markey and their eight children of Rt. 2 Ladoga are excited about starting a mission in Kiev, Ukraine." Was it a big sacrifice? Neither George nor any of the family considered the move to Ukraine to be a sacrifice. Having been raised on the mission field and instilled with this understanding from her parents, Pam taught her children that what they were doing was a privilege.

It was a blessed obedience. Many years later while sharing at a conference, Pam says, "My dad told us kids, 'You children are so privileged.' And you know, I grew up believing that. I believed that I was blessed and I watched their lives, and they served the Lord as if it were a privilege."

Joy is found in contentment. George and Pam believed that this understanding is vital for any family serving on the foreign mission field. They believed that if a missionary family moves to the field believing that what they are doing is a huge sacrifice, or, if while on the field they are entertaining in their minds thoughts about what they do not have and what they or their children are not experiencing, they will ultimately lose any sense of joy and blessing that can come from being there. In fact, if children are discontented on the mission field, perhaps it is because they see a lack of contentment in their parents. Pam continues, "It can be such a temptation to feel sorry for yourself, to fall into a pit of self-pity, especially when we listen to the voices around us. But we're not this poor little group suffering so the Gospel can go forth. We are called. We are privileged. We are together. We are united."

THE DREAM OF A LITTLE GIRL

On June 29, Pam's parents, John and Marjorie Pemberton arrived at the farmhouse. John, with his years of missionary experience, wisdom, and booming voice, spoke to each of the children words of challenge, blessing, and encouragement. Marjorie chimed in as well, reminding Pam of a story that she had long forgotten. Years before when Pam was a little girl, the following conversation had taken place. "Mommy, Daddy, I want to go to the Soviet Union," said Pamela Pemberton while growing up in Southern Rhodesia. "People there need to hear about Jesus." "That's nice, Pammy," replied her mother. At the young age of 12, Pam had felt that she wanted to be a missionary when she grew up, but to do so she felt that it had to be a hard life (as if Africa was not hard enough). "I thought to myself, where would be the hardest place, the most dangerous place in the world?" Pam says. "Immediately I thought of the Soviet Union. I wanted to go there and witness to Khrushchev."

But for the next 30 years, the dream of that little girl was placed on hold. Pam continues, "By the time Rhonda, our fourth child, was born in the early eighties, I had come to the understanding that I would probably never return to the mission field, but that perhaps my children would. My job then became to prepare them for all that God had for them, even becoming missionaries." However, now her childhood dream of returning to the mission field, even that specific ambition of venturing into the lands of the former Soviet Union, was becoming a reality.

With her parents now spending longer periods of time in the States due to health problems, after almost 40 years of life and ministry in Zimbabwe, it had been difficult for Pam to share the news with them that it was now their daughter and their grandchildren who would be moving away. Although saddened on hearing the news, knowing that they would not be seeing their daughter and grandchildren for some time, Pam's parents got behind the family, encouraging them in their preparations for the trip. Pam says, "My dad was the quintessential packer. When he and Mom came up, he helped us get all of the bags together. My dad took Rhonda, our daughter who was twelve at the time, and discipled her in how to pack. We ended up with thirty-five bags – two large ones for each person plus a carry-on, and a few more thrown in." The remaining days included many heartfelt goodbyes to family and close friends.

FAREWELL IN CHICAGO

The long line of cars escorting the Markeys to Chicago's O'Hare International Airport seemed to be a funeral procession for some, but for George and his family it was an exciting venture of faith. Feelings of excitement for a new direction and an anticipation that God was going to do something extraordinary were now sweeping over this family who was preparing to embark on this mission. All of the bags came out of the multiple vans and cars. All of the children put on their backpacks and carry-ons. "Mom told us to make it look like our carry-ons were as light as a feather so that the people at the airport would not try to weigh them," says Melanie, who was only 10 years old at the time. As they walked up to the check-in desk, it was unknown what the costs would be for the extra luggage. However, to the surprise of the family and friends standing there, all of the extra bags were put through free. Emotional farewells were said, multiple hugs given, prayers and correspondence promised. The time came for the family to board the plane, and for the others to make the long, tearful drive back home.

THE FRENCH CONNECTION

The flight was long but without incident, that is, at least until they disembarked in France. The transfer in Paris was confusing, and the kids were tired and thirsty. When some of the kids went to find a drink, a guard motioned them behind a security cordon and out of the transit area. After purchasing beverages, they were not permitted back into the transit area to the rest of the family. Shut off, unable to communicate, the kids did the only thing they could: They found a way to sneak back through the security cordon. Finally together, they began to look for the departure gate. Finally after receiving conflicting information from various airport employees, the Markeys made it to their gate only to find that the flight had been overbooked. Having heard horror stories about Russian airlines, the Markeys were hesitant to board their only remaining option, an Aeroflot flight. However, once they were on board, the change in planes turned out to be a blessing in disguise. Pam writes, "It turned out well because we could take all of our carry-ons, put them on the seats beside us, lay the seats down in front of us, and put our legs up—never mind safety and service!" George was 50 years old, Pam 44, and his children ranged in ages from 16 years old to 6 months old when they made their journey to Ukraine.

INDEPENDENCE DAY

Flying into Kiev on July 4, 1992, was an unforgettable experience. As the wheels of the plane touched down, dilapidated shacks, old planes, and trees and overgrown bushes surrounding the airport seemed to race by. Thuds were felt every second as the plane rode over the concrete slabs that had been laid down for a runway. The tall grass growing up in between these concrete slabs left one wondering how many flights actually arrived into this airport. Eventually the plane came to a stop at the Borispol International Terminal.

Upon exiting the plane, the family discovered that looking for a baggage carousel was an effort in futility. While pondering the status of their belongings, the Markeys and everyone else from the plane were herded into an empty room and left standing and wondering. Soon the sound of a tractor jolted everyone into alertness. Gazing around the room, local people soon began to congregate around an open area in the middle of the room. The sound of the tractor grew louder and then finally emerged from the back of the room. Behind the tractor was hitched a trailer, and on the trailer was a huge mound of luggage. Before the tractor even came to a halt, people from the plane were climbing up onto the trailer and hunting for their luggage. As the engine of the tractor finally shut down, George climbed onto the trailer and began searching for their belongings, passing them to his children. All of the bags were gathered and the family was once again left standing and wondering. A line was forming, meandering into a dark corridor over to their left. The all-important matter of lines would be something that the Markeys would learn over time. For now, the 10 family members got into line, amazed at the pushing, shoving, and trampling as people rushed to cut in front of them. To their right stood a small glass-encased display cabinet offering "duty free" items, and to which no one seemed to be paying attention. A solitary light bulb dangling over their heads was the only source of a dim and insufficient illumination to the path before them.

After passing through customs, the family followed the other passengers to a set of doors. As the doors opened, all that could be seen was a wall of humanity. The passengers ahead of them walked directly into this mass of people, and as they did, a small crevice emerged through which they then inched forward. Not wanting to miss out on their chance, George led the charge, the people in the crowd seemingly not phased by the commotion, elbows, and other body parts clashing into each other. Any apologies offered for bags rolling over shoes went unanswered by people who were returning only empty stares and confused expressions.

Upon exiting the terminal at night, the family stood around in the darkness feeling as though they had entered the Twilight Zone. They were tired and hungry from their trip, overwhelmed by the newness of their surroundings, and still dazed from the trampling they had just endured. Sasha Andreashina, a member of the church that had invited George during his earlier trip, met the family at the airport. Sasha remembers, "I was shocked seeing such a large family, and only had seen Americans one other time before." With a rudimentary knowledge of English, Sasha greeted the family and brought them to the hotel that they would call home for the next couple of months.

CHAPTER SIXTEEN

LIFE, PEOPLE, AND MINISTRY IN KIEV

Boasting a population of three million people, Kiev was the largest city in which George and the family had ever lived. Situated on the Dnieper River, the capital of Ukraine had grown to include both sides of the river. With its green, tree-lined boulevards, parks and historical sites, universities and museums, Kiev was a beautiful, intriguing city, and the family was anxious to explore it. However, more than anything else, they were interested in meeting the people. Living in a hotel near the center of the city afforded them the opportunity to meet new people on a daily basis, as well as to easily travel throughout the city.

Upon arrival at the hotel, Pam doled out any leftovers that she had collected from the various flights. It was only in the early hours of the morning in Ukraine when they finally were able to go to sleep. The next morning, Pam remembers, "Our first meal consisted of bread and Coke. We tore off chunks, dipped it into Coke, and then ate it. Then that evening we ate what was left of the bread, dipping it into Kool-Aid." In the following days, the discovery of a cafeteria in the hotel enabled them to eat until they could find out how to shop. As time went on, the Markeys soon began to learn where grocery stores were located, how to exchange money, and how to navigate through the purchasing process. Unable to verbally communicate with the impatient store clerks, the Markeys were reduced to pointing and grunting to indicate which products they wanted behind the counters.

Then, in order to make any purchase in a store, they had to first wait in a line to get a receipt for the product, move to another line to pay for it and receive a new receipt, and only then get into a third line to pick up the product. Also, they soon discovered that shopping bags were not provided at the stores. Pam remembers, "Whoever went out always took bags with them just in case they happened to find a place selling something that we could use." Furthermore, stores did not have a consistent supply of food, so to go shopping with a list was a quick route to disappointment. In the wake of the collapse of the Soviet centralized economy, important staples such as flour, cheese, sugar, and milk would disappear for days and weeks at a time. George and Pam encouraged the family to make it a daily adventure to see where stores and markets were located, what new foods could be discovered, and where necessities like toilet paper, laundry detergent, and light bulbs could be found.

Melanie says, "Dad's attitude was always positive. He really set the tone for all of our attitudes. He was really sensitive to what we said or did. He wanted us to be sensitive to the culture, to the people. I remember that Rhonda and I started being picky about the food. I remember Dad coming over to us and he was really firm, saying, 'We are going to eat everything on our plate. We are not going to leave anything. That is polite. We don't want to offend anyone. That's the polite way to do things.' After that, whatever was put in front of us, we never complained; we always ate it. I even remember seeing a dog walking into the restaurant. Things didn't seem very clean or anything, but our parents never complained. Since they were not complaining, we learned to take things as they came, and that it was an adventure."

Although the number of mice that the family caught in their hotel room is a matter of dispute, everyone remembers that it was mouse number 14 that George Robert smashed under his boot to the resounding applause of the family and the loving admiration of his father. Melanie continues, "We just kind of took every challenge as they came. Dad really encouraged us to do that." Sasha, who had met them at the airport, says, "Only years later did we even know that the Markeys were practically starving when they came, that they did not have water in their hotel, and that their rooms were infested with mice. They never talked about it in front of us. They never complained."

However, the transition did seem to affect certain family members more than others. Soon after arriving in Ukraine, George Robert became severely depressed, even to the point of having panic attacks. Pam writes, "Georgie is in tears this morning. Depressed, can barely function." The next day, she records, "Georgie worries so much. He has had a true panic attack. Such fear. I held him in my arms while he wept. Mostly it is anxiety for the future." A few days later she continues writing, especially about how they were dealing with the depression. "The children are doing so well. Georgie talked with George and me for at least an hour last night. We shared with him of our experiences of difficult times in our lives, and how God used them and brought us through. It was so good. It was the first time all of us have sat down and had such an excellent talk." It soon became clear that adapting to life in Ukraine would be a process.

MEETING THE PEOPLE

True ministry begins long before we realize it. Although intent on learning the language of the people, as any missionary should be, the Markeys soon realized that it did not take a previous knowledge of the Russian or Ukrainian languages to be communicators of the Gospel. They were under a microscope—people observing them, their lives, attitudes, and actions. Pam writes in her journal dated July 11, "Still no water in the hotel. I never imagined how much the Lord was training me in the early years in Zimbabwe for such a time as this. We came home this evening hot, sticky, and so dirty. I thought, 'How will we be prepared tomorrow to go to church?'" Finding a spring outside, George began pumping water and hauling it up to the family in the hotel. Pam continues, "Of course, you know George. He didn't just carry water for us, but for half of the people in the hotel. Some Armenians down the hall were so impressed with him that they invited him to come in and asked him all kinds of questions."

The following day was their first Sunday in Kiev, and the Markeys attended the Good News church, the church that had invited them to Ukraine. Although they had been expected to begin ministering in this church upon their arrival, what they discovered that Sunday made them hesitant to fill the new role for which they had come. For, in the two short months since George's earlier visit in the spring, the Good News church had become divided over some key issues. The issue most concerning to George was the division over whether the church should have a foreign pastor. When

George realized that this was the case, he immediately thanked the church for their invitation, but declined any involvement in the church. He was not about to be the reason for a division within a church, and he believed that if there was a national who could pastor, he should be encouraged to do so. Furthermore, that particular Sunday, a hyper-charismatic group from Australia had arrived and was permitted to share at the church. What took place during that service left the Markeys questioning the very foundations of this church. With a message and service based completely on emotions and experience, George and his family walked out even before the service was over.

More and more, George could see that there was a huge need for a church that would simply teach the Word of God. A growing problem was becoming more and more evident. Arriving to attempt to fill the spiritual vacuum of post-communism were not only missionaries who were evangelizing and teaching the Bible, but also deviant Christian groups seemingly interested in fleecing the flock of God, as well as blatantly cultic groups desiring to spread their tentacles into the hearts of the Ukrainian people. Although many good church teams and evangelistic groups were coming, few were choosing to stay and be involved in any significant way. In the early 1990s, various teams could be seen in the central square of Kiev, singing, preaching, and evangelizing. However, during these outreaches, on the fringes of the crowds were hovering Mormon missionaries, Jehovah's Witnesses, Hare Krishnas, and others who were more than willing to snatch up those who had "professed Christ," but who were then deserted after the departure of the short-term teams. "Where are the pastors?" The question began growing in George's heart, and would become an irritant in the ears of many back home in the States as George would frequently ask it.

There were several missionary groups, and even two other Calvary Chapel missionaries, in Ukraine when George arrived, but they were mostly involved in humanitarian projects and evangelistic outreaches. Since none of them were pastors, they were not interested in planting a church, but were content to funnel people into local congregations, even those congregations whose foundations were somewhat questionable in their integrity or consistency in adhering to biblical truth. After talking with George about what was happening at the Good News church, one of these missionaries encouraged George to begin his own Sunday-morning service.

As they continued to seek the Lord about the possibility of beginning a new fellowship, the Markeys persevered in their attempts to get to know people, share Jesus with them, and further immerse themselves in the language and culture of Ukraine.

Relatively few cars traveled the wide city streets because most people utilized the vast public transportation system consisting of metros (subways), buses, trams, and trolleys. From the Bolshevik metro station near their hotel, the kids ventured daily throughout the city, going on outings with their new friends, visiting the "water park" on the river, or even teaching softball to groups of kids. A weekly women's Bible study in the nearby cancer hospital was already being taught by Pam, and interpreted by Sasha. George had begun teaching a Bible study at Poly-technical University. Day by day they were meeting new people, sharing their lives and their faith, and working on the language. Pam writes, "Working on Russian is slow and painful. Sometimes it seems like we work forever on just one word."

THE CHERNOBYL NUCLEAR DISASTER

One day while riding the metro, the family met a man by the name of Anatoli. Himself affected by the radiation from the Chernobyl nuclear disaster which had occurred only six years earlier, Anatoli had been told simply to drink red wine in order to flush the deadly radiation from his body. Another of Pam's new acquaintances, Lilly, further described this tragic "accident" to her. In her journal, Pam quotes Lilly as saying, "We live in a giant prison." As the Markeys met with Anatoli, Lilly, and others, they soon learned more about the tragic nuclear "accident," and the ensuing coverup, and they began to understand how little concern there had been among the leaders of the Soviet Union for the inhabitants of this now-fractured empire.

On April 26, 1986, a series of malfunctions led to a meltdown at the nuclear power plant located near the city of Chernobyl, some 60 miles from Kiev. Nearby was Pripyat, a city of about 5,000 people and home to most of the employees working at the plant. Its inhabitants were preparing for the upcoming May Day celebrations, walking with their babies in the streets, children playing soccer outside in the fresh spring air. The time for planting their gardens was right around the corner. However, little did they know that the bright glow on the skyline was something other than the setting sun.

For many days after the accident, the people of Ukraine were not informed of the dangers they were facing, nor were they told of the simple remedies that could help stave off some of the most critical health issues. The leaders of the Soviet Union maintained a tight grip on the release of any information about what was actually happening at the nuclear facility, themselves sending away their own families to other cities or nations abroad. The invisible poison was being driven into the populated city of Kiev on trucks that were being hosed down and sent back to battle the fires at the Chernobyl plant. Conscripted soldiers were told that if they would work for two minutes battling the fires, they would be exempted from their mandatory two years of military service. Neighboring Scandinavian countries were the first to report the radioactive clouds making their way toward large portions of northern Europe. And yet, the people of Ukraine were told nothing. Pam writes, "No one ever told them not to eat the food or drink the water." In fact, the news of the tragedy first broke in the West and was broadcast over shortwave radio into the Soviet Union. Quoting Lilly, Pam writes, "We first heard about what had happened at Chernobyl by an American radio broadcast that we secretly received on shortwave radio."

Cancers, miscarried pregnancies, thyroid problems, and other illnesses would plague an entire generation of Ukrainians, searing into their minds and hearts the painful reality of a system filled with self-absorbed, corrupt, and delusional leaders. I remember how frequently people spoke of Chernobyl in those early years, especially when someone was sick. The lead singer of the new Ukrainian Christian music group Seven told me of his experiences as a soldier working at Chernobyl that summer. He says, "The cherries on the trees that year were as big as apples. We picked them and checked them with our devices and they were clean, so we ate them. But after that year, those trees did not bear any more fruit." He further described how his own immune system was totally destroyed by the radiation. "I can get a small cut on my toe and my whole foot will swell up because my body cannot fight the infection."

The Chernobyl disaster, World War II, the forced starvations and indiscriminate liquidations under Stalin, and centuries of servitude as the pawns in other nations' chess games were all national tragedies that were imbedded in the psyche of these now-independent Ukrainian people. They were a people who had endured much suffering, seemingly everyone with a story of pain, loss, despair, or death. Memories that earlier had been spoken only behind closed doors were now beginning to emerge, painting a dark picture over the shining facade of Soviet realism. Furthermore, the recent collapse of a political and ideological system to which most had pledged their allegiance had injected their souls with even greater doses of despondency. Entire life savings were completely devalued in a matter of a few short days and weeks. Formerly stable-paying jobs were now remunerating their employees in the wares of what they produced – sausage from the sausage factory, clothes from the clothing factory, or even toilet paper from the toilet paper factory. Barter and bazaars became the means of survival during this time of an untrusted past, an unstable present, and an unknown future.

Amazingly, just as a battered wife, numb to any other alternative, frequently desires to return to an abusive husband, so many Ukrainians longed for the past when at least they could afford sausage, had free vacations, and were guaranteed jobs. Never mind such frivolous things as care for life, human rights, consideration, dignity, and freedom of thought, opinion, and religion. Seemingly beaten into compliance, the people could retreat only into the solitude of their minds. On public transport, it was despairing to see the empty eyes of the people, either looking off into the distance or down at the ground. Women walking down the streets were wearing similar dresses, having few options available to them in the stores. Everyone had been taught they should be equal, and now all were equally miserable. They were a people with nowhere else to turn, and it was in this dark and tumultuous time that the hope of the Gospel of Jesus Christ was beginning to take root in the hearts of a downcast and dejected people.

THE GOSPEL AND CHURCH POLITICS

The Gospel of Jesus Christ is the power of God to salvation for everyone who believes (Rom. 1:16). Irrespective of cultural background or ethnicity, indifferent to economic status or political persuasion, and independent of forced godlessness or staunch tradition, the wonderful news of this free forgiveness and salvation available in Jesus was now being proclaimed in Ukraine.

As new relationships were being formed and people were coming to know Jesus, George made the decision to begin a new fellowship of believers.

The two other Calvary Chapel missionaries who were serving in Kiev were vocally supportive of George's decision, reaffirming that they were not called to be pastors. The first Sunday service was held on July 26, just a few short weeks after their arrival. However, the beginnings of this church would not be without conflict. Pam, recording an entry in her journal on that day, writes, "The first day of the start of Calvary Chapel in Kiev. A day of intense pain, grief, rejection." What should have been a time of celebration was actually being subverted by the same man who had organized George's first trip to Russia and Ukraine back in May.

Evangelistic teams were being brought in from Calvary Chapels in southern California and elsewhere by this leader. Other American missionaries were coming down from Moscow as well, and outreaches were taking place in parks and various places around the city. It was encouraging to see people place their trust in Jesus, their lives being changed. However, it soon became apparent that something was not right. Two of George's older children, George Robert and Robin, were sitting in the cafeteria of the hotel one day when a short-term team from California came in to eat. Without knowing that it was George's children who were sitting at a nearby table, the subject of that team's conversation soon began to focus on George Markey, and it quickly turned very negative. George and Robin remember hearing these men speak about their dad in this slanderous way, and were very confused by it—for these American pastors and leaders had not even met their father, and the things they were saying were untrue and almost hateful. They were sharing things that they had heard from the man who was leading their team, saying that they had been told by him not to speak with George or his family, that George was not going to be the pastor of a church in Kiev. As the kids told their dad of this conversation, what happened next astonished them even more. The next time the family saw this leader, he excitedly walked up to George and his family, warmly informing his team that "this is George Markey and his wonderful family." A clap on the back in front of everyone seemed to show his friendship, but behind George's back, malicious lies and hate seemed to seep out of his mouth. Some of the American missionaries who were visiting from Moscow saw what was taking place and encouraged George to keep going.

Over a period of time, George would receive many phone calls from other pastors in Russia and Belarus who were also having difficult encounters with this American leader. As George began to investigate, what became clear was that this man had been taking American teams throughout former Soviet republics in order to help plant churches. However, if this man did not approve of the missionaries who were already serving there, meaning that he did not think that they would submit to his controlling leadership, then he would supplant those missionaries by starting his own church nearby, stealing those missionaries' local workers, and installing foreign or local pastors of his choosing. Not only those in Russia, Belarus, and now Ukraine, but other missionaries in Poland, Hungary, Austria, and the Czech Republic were reporting damaging run-ins with this visiting leader. It seemed that conflict, contention, confusion, and waves of destruction were the most enduring aftereffects of this man's work. Even more difficult to understand was the fact that this situation was not being dealt with by those who were responsible for this American leader in the States.

As for now, the plan unfolding in front of their eyes was obvious, hurtful. The hypocrisy and lies that were coming from this man's mouth were unbearable. The lack of moral and spiritual support was discouraging. Pam writes, "We came to Ukraine as missionaries. Echoing in our ears were the words, 'You go and we will support you,' and, 'We are sending our best.' Now we are here and it is confusing what we are doing, and with whom. It came out that [this leader] is bringing another group in 2½ weeks to start a different Calvary Chapel, and he is certainly not of a mind to support us. I am so sick at heart at this time. It is all so wretchedly depressing. God help us." When that next team did arrive from the States, through the counsel of their leader, pastors from that group ordained, supported, and established one of the other two Calvary Chapel missionaries who were living in Kiev—a missionary who had said that he was not called to pastor. Only years later would it be discovered that this new "pastor" was extorting churches in America and the body of Christ in Ukraine, bringing disrepute on the name of Jesus. In time, he would be quietly removed from Ukraine and sent back to the U.S. for restoration, the leaders in the States who had ordained this man into the ministry later apologizing to George Markey for their error.

But for now, the confusion continued. In what became a frequent occurrence, those Ukrainians working with George would be called by the other "pastor" for assistance in interpretation or ministry, and then somehow would begin working only with him. George always let them go—for he refused to use fleshly means or manipulation to motivate someone to work with him. But, at the same time, George could not sit still while such divisive practices were being allowed to continue. Phone calls were made back to the States, and other visiting pastors and leaders returned to their churches as vocal witnesses to the devious, treacherous, and hypocritical activities of this visiting leader and his hastily installed puppet-pastor. The answer to these claims, nothing. The result of this inaction, further confusion. In response, George decided to call Pastor Chuck Smith. "I will change the name of the church if I have to," George said. "I am not concerned about making a name for myself or any organization. I will not tolerate this interference of American church politics with the Gospel of Jesus Christ. I am concerned about the unity of the Body of Christ. And this man is an evil liar and a deceiver—he is sowing discord wherever he goes. If he is allowed to work in Ukraine, then I will change the name of the church." The reaction from the States was the restricting of the area of this devious man's missionary activity, forbidding him to work in Ukraine and allowing him to continue only in Russia.

With all of this conflict surrounding the decision to begin a church in Kiev, other opportunities for ministry began to look very enticing. George had been contacted by Steve Weber of the Christian Broadcasting Network (CBN) about starting a work in the Russian city of Chelyabinsk. Having been informed that there were more than 4,000 believers in Chelyabinsk who needed a pastor, George and Pam began to prayerfully consider this option. Amid the chaos and hurt, writing in her journal Pam shares that they were beginning to wonder whether they had misheard or overstepped what the Lord had for them. "Perhaps these are just my feelings, but then this situation of Chelyabinsk came up and we felt it might be the answer." Only after the collapse of communism did the extent of the multiple nuclear disasters and radioactive dumps near this formerly closed city begin to be revealed. The extensive pollution to the river, the nuclear waste put into the lake, and ensuing radioactive dust would affect more than 500,000 people, leading some to name Chelyabinsk "the most contaminated spot on the planet." Pam shares, "I had great hope when George went to meet Steve Weber. I thought it would be good to become a part of some stable organization and leave the madness behind. It was not like George to be put off by some kind of physical hardship, but he would say, 'Do you know how much radiation is there? More than Chernobyl.' I hated the conflict going on in Kiev, worse than death, and I was somewhat depressed after George did not take the invitation." But after days of prayer, and this meeting with Steve Weber, George made the decision on August 5 that they would stay in Kiev.

LOOKING FOR A NEW PLACE

With the decision to stay came the beginning of the harvest of souls. After one Sunday service in early August, eight people prayed to commit their lives to Jesus. Immediately after the service, the young church marched down to the Dnieper River for baptisms. New people were coming into the Markeys' lives daily. A veterinarian student from Ethiopia named Job became a constant companion, radiating the love of Jesus and serving others. Other university students, teachers, doctors, musicians, members of the Academy of Science, all were coming to meet the Markeys and hear George preach about Jesus. Next began the adventure of finding a new meeting place for Sunday-morning services. August 16 was the first Sunday that they met in the Conservatory of Music, located on the central square of the city. However, because of frequent music practices or concerts on Sundays, the hall that had been promised to them would often be unavailable, this information discovered only when they would arrive for services. While alternating Sundays between the Museum of Lenin, the Conservatory, and another music school, George began to look for other meeting places, as well as other housing opportunities. Up to this point, while living out of their carry-ons and longing for a more permanent living arrangement, the suitcases that the Markeys had arrived with from America were still packed.

"He was apartment hunting for a really long time," shares Melanie. "Since we were in that hotel, I know that it was on his mind to get us a place to live. But it was really hard to find an apartment that would house ten people." After inquiring among local pastors about which area of the city was the most unreached, George made the decision to move to Teremki, a large region on the southern side of Kiev. He was told that there were many families and larger apartments in that area of the city. However, when he searched, the only place he could find in this region was a "hotel" on the seventh floor of an apartment building. Four separate rooms were allotted to the Markeys for the price of about $15 each per month. Soon after the move, new workers from the church in Crawfordsville, Diana Faulk, Greg Sabens, and I, began to arrive, living on the opposite end of the same "hotel" floor. On the day I flew into Kiev, I remember driving up in a taxi to this building with multiple suitcases only to find the elevator not working.

Even though the family and team were living in Teremki, Sunday-morning services were still being held in the center of the city. On Sunday mornings, finding enough room on a bus or trolley going into the city was not difficult since, for most people, it was their day off. Carrying kids, instruments, and sound equipment, we made the long, weekly trips to the Conservatory. But after a few Sundays it became apparent that it was very difficult to maintain a consistent group of people in such a transient part of the city. Since we were living in the southern region of the city, George began looking for a large hall somewhere closer to home.

Meanwhile, immediately after the move to Teremki, Bible studies began at the auditorium of school #132, which was located directly behind the apartment building. Because of their need for funds, area schools seemed very open to the idea of renting out their auditoriums in the evenings, even for religious purposes. Also, it seemed that everyone wanted to learn English, and the teachers and parents at this school and others were more than willing to provide classrooms where their children could attend English lessons taught by a native English speaker, even if the Bible was being used as the textbook. Soon, schools throughout the region began opening their doors, resulting in an abundance of opportunities for teaching students English using the Bible during the day, and then holding multiple Bible studies in the evenings.

After a few weeks of searching for a meeting place, George found a nearby movie theater named Zagreb, after the famous city in former Yugoslavia, which agreed to rent out their hall for Sunday-morning services. Zagreb was a building that we passed every day on our way into the city center, directly on the main road. With very few movie theaters in the area, everyone knew about Zagreb. Having both a small and a large hall, as well as a cafeteria and rooms that we could use for Sunday school and youth group, Zagreb was much larger than what we needed at the time. But George was always looking beyond. He believed that it was important to meet in a place that not only would be centrally located for easy access, but also would demonstrate his faith that God wanted to do great things in many lives. After contacting the organization Campus Crusade for Christ, we were loaned a movie-theater version of the Jesus film in Russian to use. The plan was to have two showings of the movie on Friday and Saturday nights, inviting anyone who was interested to come to the first church service the following Sunday. Advertisements were made and hung at bus stops, posted on street poles, and handed out on the street. The result was two nights filled with excitement as people crowded the hall, watching the story of Jesus for the first time in their lives. George introduced the movie, and then there was an altar call afterward. Dozens of people came forward to receive Jesus. In our naiveté, with Bibles, tracts, and other literature on hand to distribute, the offer was made for anyone who wanted a free Bible to come forward. As I stood at the front of the hall, I was not prepared for the mass of people rushing toward me. I was soon overwhelmed, overrun, and overlooked, as pleading hands forcefully reached into the bags in order to snatch whatever they could find. Yes, there was spiritual hunger, but there was also a desire to grab something that was "free." We soon learned to distribute materials and assistance with a little more wisdom.

Sons and daughters, mothers and fathers, grandmothers and grandfathers soon began coming. As one person found the hope of life, soon they began to invite friends and family, coworkers, and fellow students to come with them to this young church. Older people would frequently say, "It may be too late for me, but I want my children to go." Others came because they wanted to see what their children were doing, or what, supposedly, was being done to them. Various labels were thought up in order to stigmatize this new church. But whether the church was labeled a venomous sect, a brainwashing cult, or an institution preying on weak-minded people, the truth was that lives were changing. Soon after we had moved into this new meeting place, 29 people were baptized at an indoor swimming pool behind Zagreb. Others wanted to be baptized, but their parents would not yet permit them. Lena Voloshina, one of the many students who came to Jesus during this time, shares, "In the early '90s there were many sects that would encourage children to go against their parents, like the White Brotherhood group. Sometimes I would be upset with my parents for not letting me go out and do things with the church, and I would complain to people in church. But George and Pam never criticized our parents. Never. They never said, 'Oh, they just don't understand because they are not believers.' They never gave any counsel that pitted me against my parents.

But, rather, they were patient and prayed, and encouraged us to obey our parents in every way. The result was that our parents grew in their respect and appreciation for George and Pam, and for the Lord as they saw changes in our lives."

SCHOOL, NEW FRIENDSHIPS, RICH FELLOWSHIP

That autumn, George and Pam enrolled their children in local public schools for a few hours each day, specifically for the purpose of learning and practicing the Russian language. Jon Markey, who began kindergarten the year of their move, shares, "I remember kids making fun of me from the very beginning. It started in kindergarten. Not being able to speak the language, and when you start to learn a language you make mistakes. Russian grammar is very complicated, and kids are very unforgiving in that way. You make a mistake and they think it is hilarious." As for Pam, she was able to find a private language tutor whom she would visit three times a week, while leaving little Aaron in the care of Diana Faulk. Soon, Pam and the kids became more and more functional in the language, able to read, write, and speak it. George, on the other hand, never seemed to let the dust settle enough for him to adequately study and learn the language. For me, I had the fortune of spending almost every day with George, and it was a chore to keep up with him as he ran around the city with all of his dynamic energy, bursting zeal, and love of life. George Robert, who had gone through bouts of depression and anxiety, found language partners, and he learned Russian well enough that people thought he was a native speaker. As the official language in the country changed, Ukrainian quickly became the language used in schools and universities. The Markey kids soon adapted to the change and started learning Ukrainian as well.

As the children began to make friends at school, and as students from the English classes became more and more interested in having a relationship with Jesus, fellowship took on an almost "Book of Acts" appearance. It became a daily occurrence to have guests, especially students, coming up to the apartments in which we were living. After we made the fortunate find of a 100-pound bag of Indiana popcorn, every evening turned into a time of fellowship around popcorn and tea. George knew that these times were important for those who were inquiring about our faith, or desiring to grow in their own. Yana Mospanenko was a student at school #132 and remembers, "George was so generous, always generous. I remember when he first came here, how willing he was to share their food, even American peanut butter. Actually, one time we came to visit after Bible study and he must have been sleeping, but he told us to come in and he shared with us. That meant a lot to me. Sometimes people can receive you and say, 'OK, you came here, so come on in,' but in their attitudes they are really telling you that it would be better for you to leave as fast as you can. But George was not like that. He was so open, he was so free, and in his presence you felt so comfortable."

However, the frequent lack of privacy soon became a missed luxury. Pam writes, "I feel starved for privacy. I want so much to have a small room to go where I can be renewed, nurse Aaron, weep, write, study, or cry – ALONE. Life here is so public." Pam shares about one evening in particular that went beyond anything else they had experienced. After all of the guests had left and the kids had been put to bed, George and Pam finally got settled onto their mattresses on the floor of their room. "George was already sleeping, and I was just about to doze off, when I felt this presence towering over us. I was startled and woke George up. It turned out to be one of the guys from the church who had been there earlier that evening. He said, 'Excuse me, please, I have one more question.'" And so they got up and the fellowship continued.

Open lives. I can imagine the passage from Acts 20 became very poignant to them that day: "You know, from the first day that I came to Asia, in what manner I always lived among you,...how I kept back nothing that was helpful, but proclaimed it to you, and taught you publicly and from house to house..." Spent lives. As George said, "If you abandon your will and ambition to the Lord, it is surprising what He may show you and what He may do." Paul the Apostle wrote to the Corinthians, "And I will very gladly spend and be spent for your souls..." (II Cor. 12:15). Rich lives. The relationships formed during those first years would be some of the most joyous times of ministry, seeing people come to know Jesus. In fact, these "kids" would become the core of the church. Similar to how the Apostle Paul described the Philippian believers as "my beloved and longed-for brethren, my joy and crown," so it was with these new believers (Phil. 4:1).

As these friends of George's children continued to come, it became obvious that what some had said would be a detriment to ministry on the mission field was in fact becoming a blessing, just as Pam's father had so accurately predicted. George shared about this, saying, "In 1992, a lot of people thought that we were crazy, taking eight children to Ukraine. But it has been the most beautiful experience of our lives. My children's lives have been enriched on the mission field. I don't think they will ever be comfortable anywhere else. Furthermore, my children are an essential part of our ministry team. They are a living witness for the Lord Jesus Christ."

CHAPTER SEVENTEEN

YEARS OF SOWING, MODELING, LEARNING, GROWING

IN THE WARM AUTUMN weather, evenings were sometimes spent playing simple games like kick-the-can. Life was much simpler. Activities did not revolve around television, movies, and video games, but group activities, strolls through parks and museums, birthday parties, and even trips to the ballet. Weekends involved softball, basketball, volleyball, and other activities. Having heard of American baseball, but having never seen it, crowds of young people would follow us out to a field in the middle of a forest, laughing as they swung and missed or exuberant as they hit a home run.

Sunday was a special time of fellowship, often lasting all day. From the moment people came into the hall, George felt it was necessary that they be greeted warmly. As he so often did in the States, George would inquire about the person's family, their studies, their job, their life. Louder than life, he would laugh with such joy over the victories in peoples' lives. With compassion and abounding love, he would hug and pray for those going through times of struggle. The worship was simple, led by Pam and the teenagers who had just recently come to Christ.

After the service was over and all of the equipment taken down and stored, only then did the exodus from the theater begin. People loved to stay around to visit and ask questions. In the early years, one of the effects of the deplorable state of the Ukrainian economy, and the ever-changing dollar-to-coupon exchange rate, was that an entire three-course meal at a restaurant could be purchased for less than one dollar. Often after church, the Markeys and groups of upwards of 10 or 20 other people from church would go to the Jockey restaurant. Perhaps a result of the economy, but also partially the result of the culture, most restaurants at that time did not have many clients. So when 20 or 30 people would show up at a restaurant on a Sunday afternoon to eat, and not for a drunken wedding celebration, it was quite a shock to the staff at the restaurants. Reminiscent of the days at Wendy's in Crawfordsville, George would make sure that everyone was able to find a seat, that each person had the opportunity to order, and that people had a good time of fellowship. Discussions would touch on the message that was shared that day, on Russian words that were new to the family, on school, on sharing one's faith, or on how family members who did not know the Lord were doing. Often conversations would turn to music and worship. It soon became apparent that some of the words of the songs that we were singing either did not make sense or had the wrong meaning.

Often in the evenings at the apartment, hours would be spent working on better song translations. George, always a stickler that the words we sang would have meaning and not just sound pretty, encouraged Pam to get a group of translators together and pore over the songs that we were currently singing, making any changes when needed. New songs were beginning to be translated. "Music should move people," George would often say. "Worship means 'kiss towards' in the original language. When we worship, we are showing our affection to the One who is supremely worthy of all attention, honor, and glory."

TRIAL AND ERROR

With an eagerness to see things take off, sometimes decisions were made that we would only later come to realize were not the best. When George met a young married couple who were professional musicians, he invited them to church. Hoping that they would learn about Jesus and make a decision to follow Him, George allowed them to play and even lead out in song on Sunday mornings. Although at first excited at the thought of the people in our church learning from professionals, George soon came to realize that, in spite of the good music and voices, something was missing. Worship is a spiritual act, not merely an artistic expression of one's inner beliefs and values. "I came to see how important it was that anyone who was involved in ministry was Spirit-filled," George shared. At a conference he also said, "Earlier we looked for gifted people; now we look for people filled with the Holy Spirit. They will not be true witnesses until they are filled with the Holy Spirit."

George was more concerned with the work standing still, or in getting mired in the status quo, than he was in making a mistake. Always looking beyond, George saw the best in individuals, thought of the potential for the kingdom of God as he would meet with certain individuals, and took active risks in areas where most would have passively waited for something else. Ringing in the ears of those who knew him is the phrase he often said, "Let's try it. Let's see what God wants to do."

VISITORS FROM "HOME"

It was in November of 1992 when the first team came. Pastor Bill Goodrich and a group from Horizon Christian Fellowship in Indianapolis came to Ukraine for a time of outreaches and encouragement. Their arrival not only signaled a commitment to supporting George and the work in Ukraine, but also forged a partnership that would lead to teams traveling to Ukraine almost every year. George was excited to lead the group around Kiev. George was about as American as anyone could be, and as a result, he knew how to share about the cultural challenges and differences with the American teams.

In remembering that first trip to Ukraine, Pastor Bill shares, "The first time that I was going to be involved in a street outreach, I stayed up all night preparing a message to preach in the metro. I had never done that before. God used George in a way of 'firsts' in my life." Whether on the streets in the city center, or underground in the metro, or before students in the schools, or before crowds of people in front of the local grocery store, the Word of life was shared publicly and the songs played were something that the people had never before heard. Many gave their lives to Jesus during this time.

Pam writes during this time, "It is so different for a group that comes over here for a short time. It is great for us to see the work through their eyes. It gives us a new sense of excitement, and for them it is also exciting.

However, I think that since they are here for only a short time, some things are different for us. They can spend their money freely and they are so open about how everything is so much cheaper. For example, we all went out to eat at a restaurant called the Intourist, and they paid for our meal. They then tipped the waiters 2500 coupons each [about $5 at a time when $30 a month was a good salary]!! I could see the eyes of [a certain young man from the church] light up. Then I began to see that these are the Americans that the people here have seen. These who are here for a short time – kind, loving Christians who can afford for a few weeks to eat out, give generously to those around them, take advantage of the cheap prices, and then they are gone. I know that we do some of the same things, but we must not flaunt it nor encourage those around us to be parasites, thus encouraging them to lust after material things."

Another team that arrived in January of 1993 was a group of Youth With A Mission (YWAM) workers from the discipleship training school in New York. Nine of the 30-person team were slated to work with us in the establishing of the new church. With a focus on evangelism, the YWAM team was gifted in sharing their faith through dramas, street outreaches, and music. Living above the family on the eighth floor of the same apartment building for several months, the YWAM team became an integral part of the early ministry there. Other YWAM teams that came later, unfortunately, were not nearly as interested in working with the church, and therefore were of limited fruitfulness. It was becoming more and more clear that, at least from George's calling and viewpoint, the most effective form of missionary activity was that which was centered around the establishment and encouragement of a local church. Evangelism was good, but where would the people go? Orphanage ministry was so needed, but what would happen to the orphans after these missionaries left the country? The promise that Jesus gave in Scripture was that "the gates of hell will not prevail against the Church." It does not say "non-governmental organization" or "ministry," but church. Furthermore, George believed that the model that is seen in the Book of Acts is the establishing of local churches, not humanitarian trips, crusades, or colleges. Those things are all good, and necessary, but when done apart from a local church, they are detached from the living body of Christ—the very means by which Jesus has promised to do His work in this world.

Years later, George would be invited to teach at a seminary in Odessa, Ukraine. Of that experience he shared, "The leadership of this seminary asked me what they were doing wrong. They said, 'For years we have been inviting the best teachers from around the world, translating the best textbooks, and giving our students the best resources and training. But when they graduate and go out, they plant dead churches. What are we doing wrong?' I told them that the most important aspect was the model, what they have seen. If they are planting dead churches, it is because that is the model of church that they have seen."

The Church is an assembly of believers called to be followers of Jesus, infused with the power of the Holy Spirit, gifted for service in a variety of ways, and is the collective recipient of the promises of God. George's conclusion: "The most effective way to see a move of God in a country is to prayerfully work toward the establishing of a local, model church from which people could be sent out to do the work of the ministry."

REGISTRATION

As the church continued to grow, the question of registration soon became the next obstacle facing the young congregation. Dissimilar to America, authorities in Ukraine encourage churches to be officially registered with the government. A list of 10 founding members of the church was drawn up and notarized, and a set of bylaws was drafted and then registered with the ministry of religion. Bureaucratic processes such as these in the former Soviet Union are never as quick, nor as easy, as they may appear on paper. Whether the result of corrupt officials looking for a bribe, or of obstructionist officials seeking to hinder something from starting with which they disagree, multiple trips to various offices, patience with officials, and overt gestures of gratitude are often required to move these processes along.

George, always a lover of coffee, was excited when Nescafé began selling cans of instant coffee in Kiev. Not merely for his own consumption, George began buying cans of coffee for others as well – school principals, teachers, and the ministry of religion. Knowing the small salaries of these employees, George understood that they would not be able to purchase it themselves. He also just loved to bless people. Walking into the government office that day with a large can of Nescafé under his arm, George was asked by an official if this was an attempt to move the church's registration documents forward. With a look of naiveté and a smile on his face, George said, "Nyet, nyet. This is just a little something for everyone in the office. We appreciate the work you are doing. Don't you like coffee?" As the secretaries looked at each other, smiles came over their faces, grateful for the acknowledgment of their services. It wasn't too long before the documents were granted for the registration of the church in Kiev.

TIMES OF REFRESHING AND RECONCILIATION

In September of 1993, the Markeys were especially blessed with the visit of Pam's parents, John and Marjorie Pemberton. Walking through the streets of Kiev, attending the church services and home Bible studies, the Pembertons were excited to see all that had happened in such a short time. For Pam, it was a special, uninterrupted time with her mom and dad. For the kids, it was exciting to be able to show them their school, friends, and to hear Grandma play and sing with her guitar. For George, it was encouraging to be able to talk with John through some of the cultural issues they were facing, and to be able to share with one of his mentors all that God was doing in this place. Traveling with the Pembertons was also Dr. Lusby, the very man who years earlier had demanded of George a written statement of faith before he would permit him to graduate from college. Now a close family friend, Dr. Lusby excitedly walked the streets of Kiev with George, acknowledging this work of God.

George frequently taught that one mark of a spiritually mature person is in how quickly they are able to forgive. I believe the Lord honored that in George's life, whether in choosing not to hold anything against the leadership of his college, or in choosing to release those who had wronged him in the division in the church in Crawfordsville or other places. And as the forgiveness was real and lasting in George's life, the Lord provided opportunities like this for reconciliation.

Soon, another opportunity was given. On a return trip to the States with his daughter Rhonda, George went to visit one of the couples in the church who had been vocal opponents of George and had been used to inspire division. Rhonda remembers, "Dad was kind of surprised that [this certain individual] suddenly apologized for everything. And then when he got it off his chest, he felt so much better that he began calling others who had been involved in the split." Soon, so many began coming over that they decided that they wanted to do something bigger. They decided to use the Sportsmen's Club one evening for a special time of reconciliation. Rhonda shares, "After a time of worship, this man got up and said, 'I think there are a lot of people who want to apologize and make things right,' and people began coming up to the microphone, sharing, and crying." Rhonda continues, "I remember personally feeling somewhat confused. People were coming up to me and apologizing, and I really didn't know why. Mom and Dad had kept all of this from us kids. It was not something that they had discussed in front of us, and it was obviously not something that Mom and Dad were holding on to." When the time came for George to share, he really did not have any bitterness toward any of these people that he needed to unload off of his shoulders. For him, it had been an issue that had been dealt with years earlier, and left at the cross. Painful, yes. Sorrowful, yes. But it was not hindering his personal walk with the Lord, nor his relationships with people. In fact, for George it had been embraced as an experience similar to Joseph in the Old Testament: "That which you meant for evil, God has used for good" (Gen. 50:20). Pam shares, "George was delighted. When he got back from that trip he was so thrilled with that meeting, rejoicing at the opportunities that everyone had to be reunited in the love of Jesus."

Some people ask the question, "Would George have gone to Ukraine if the division in Crawfordsville had not occurred?" However, it seems that this is not the right question to ask. We do not need to seek justification for wrongdoing, nor do we need to find a reason to hold on to any kind of offense. Rather, this is a lesson to not allow ourselves to be defined by situations, no matter how difficult, damaging, and divisive. It is also a lesson to allow God to lead us, to shape us, and to cause us to be more like Christ in our attitudes, actions, and responses. George and Rhonda returned to Ukraine having witnessed the power of reconciliation that comes through forgiveness.

LIVING THE MODEL

To be a Christian is to be like Christ—to reflect Jesus' nature. The greatest commandment of Jesus was to love God and to love men (Matt. 22:37-40). Even though George struggled with the Russian language, he spoke freely in the language of love. Sasha Andreashina shares, "George really tried to learn Russian, but he had a hard time. In spite of that, I know of many

Ukrainians who did not attend church, but who knew George, respected him, and were affected by his life, even though they hardly spoke a word to him." One of the stories that Sasha shares has to do with a man who lived in the same apartment building as George. Sasha says, "I remember walking outside one day and meeting one of George's neighbors. At that time the Markeys were living on the third floor of this building, and this man lived on the tenth floor. He told me about a time when he had brought back many large bags of potatoes from his village, but the elevator wasn't working. George drove up in his van, saw him with his bags of potatoes all around, and asked him what floor he lived on. Immediately, George began putting the bags of potatoes on his shoulders and walking them up the ten flights of stairs, until they were all gone. This man wanted me to tell George 'thank you' because he had not been able to tell him." At a time and in a place where people were constantly consumed with thoughts of their own survival, and not wanting to get involved in the problems of other people, such acts of kindness were a tremendous witness.

Oleg Ignatyev lived in the same neighborhood as the Markeys. He shares, "I remember that at that time people did not trust each other very much, let alone foreigners, or new churches. They would say things like, 'We are Orthodox.' But everyone in our neighborhood knew Pastor George. My parents and many others never worried when we began attending the church, because they saw George on the streets and they could tell who he was by his life." The living example of Christ through George would have a tremendous impact on Oleg and many other young people in the region. Oleg continues, "I was always amazed at how George loved everyone around him. That was the most important thing to me. It was the greatest example of a true witness of Christ. It did not matter whether it was showing care to kids at church, or helping the grandmas that were cleaning the buildings, or helping the men at the parking garages. He loved people. For me personally, something that I will remember for my whole life happened when I was about 15 or 16. My family was rather poor and did not usually buy us much of anything. George knew about this, and whenever he came back from the States he brought new shoes for his son, David, and for me, even though I wasn't his son.

"One other time, I remember when I was about 18 and was a student at the institute. George called me and wanted to meet me downtown. It was winter and there was snow on the ground. I had been wearing somebody's old tennis shoes, because that was all I had. I met George and he took me to a store and bought me a new pair of winter boots, boots that I would wear for the next five years. And then he took me to a store where he bought me jeans. At that moment I understood the influence of Christianity was not only seen in a person's conversations about spiritual things, such as giving them information about how they should live, or about sin. But true Christianity affects a person's life and actions. When George bought those things for me, he did not tell me, 'See how God is blessing you through me,' or some other spiritual phrase like people often say. Rather, I saw that Christianity easily connects with life, and is more simple than people think. The result was that George's life affected me so much that now I want to do the same thing, to show love to people."

Stepan Mankovsky shares about his first visit to the church in Kiev: "I wasn't a Christian when I first went to church, but I liked Olenka and I wanted to see where she was going, what kind of cult this was. George greeted me at the door when I came in. I had no idea that this very pleasant guy at the entrance was the pastor. It confused me a little bit." He continues, "But when I got saved and began to spend more time with Pastor George, I realized that he was the most loving person in the world. His love was overwhelming all of the time. He knew the love of Jesus and he demonstrated the image of Jesus to everyone. He passed it on. Pastor George showed me an example of the Christian. It wasn't a one- or two-day experience, but all of his life. He taught me to love other people, and to care about those you didn't know.

"One of the things I always thought, I felt like I'm special for him. He always had time for me. He could meet me and we would have dinner or lunch, or he would spend time with me on Saturday mornings. Only now do I realize that an hour or two on Saturday mornings when you have kids is a sacrifice, but he always had time for me and the young families in the church. He helped us with everything. He took us shopping because we did not have a car. At times he paid our bills, or he would try to help as much as he could. Only later when he was gone and I started talking to other people did I notice that they said the same thing. Maybe you were one of 200 or 300 people, but you still felt special to him. There was a time when I lived with George Robert and I asked him, 'Did you or any of your brothers and sisters ever feel that you were lacking any attention when your dad is spending time with others rather than you?' He immediately said no."

George officiated Stepan and Olenka's wedding, beginning their family life in the church. Olenka shares, "Pastor George was a God-pleaser and a people-lover. He was very open but very sincere. He hardly ever cared about any social conventions. For him it was important to do what was right and good in a given situation. Rather than being concerned with what was proper to do or to say, he did what was good. He would offer little children sweets on the buses. When he was excited to see someone, he was loud and would hug them, not thinking about whether it was right or what people thought. No person was too insignificant for pastor George."

THE WORD OF GOD

A large part of the example that Ukrainians saw in George was his love for the Word of God. Sasha Andreashina shares, "He was so excited about the Lord and the Word of God. So much passion, love, joy. He could talk about the Lord and His Word without stopping. One of my favorite books to teach now is the Book of Revelation, and that is because he was always talking about it. George would share, 'Revelation is the only book of the Bible that promises a blessing to the one who reads it, hears it, and acts upon it.' Also, when he was teaching the Book of Acts, one of his favorite books, he would immediately apply it to our lives, to our church. He would say things like, 'Barnabas. Barnabas means the son of encouragement. We need more people like this in our church.' And I would sit there and think, 'I want to be like Barnabas, a person who encourages and builds up. And after every sermon I felt like, 'I am going to get up and go do something.' It was so practical, and that came from the fact that he loved God and His word, and lived it out in his own life."

Oleg Ignatyev says, "I always admired his love for the Bible. He would say things like, 'You can always check me out; I am just a man. I can say something, but you should not believe me, but check it out in the Word of God. What does it say?' To me, this was an important characteristic. I learned that the Word of God was more important than pastor George's own words."

Yana Mospanenko shares, "I learned from George about the leader, that he's not the one who rules and controls. George had a love for the people and a love for the truth. With that love he led by example. He showed me that the leader is the first one who does the work. There are no dirty jobs. Things like sweeping the floor, getting boxes, or driving." Yana continues, "One Sunday morning a group of us were going to another city for outreach. For a pastor, Sunday morning is a time to be getting ready for church and the sermon, but George met us at 4:00 am and drove us to where we needed to go. And when I told this to a friend from another church, they were shocked, because they didn't see this in their church. In other churches, the church revolved around the pastor, but George was around the church. He was supporting and loving the church in whatever way he could. And he was always reaching out to people. He always had cookies for those ladies at the door [who monitored the entrances], and he was always inviting people to go eat with him, not because he wanted something from them, but because he wanted to give—to bless them.

"But I also learned that Pastor George was very strict with the truth," Yana says. "If it was not from God, if it was not in the Bible, he would say so right away. Sometimes there were things with which I disagreed, but I had to obey, because the authority was the Word of God. George never taught us to obey him. Never. But somehow he disciplined us with his behavior, with his loving example, and his love for the truth." As the image of Christ was portrayed through the lives of His servants, the body of Christ in Kiev was being equipped for the work of the ministry (Eph. 4:12).

OTHER PASTORS, CHURCHES, AND OUTREACHES

Soon other pastors began to come to Kiev. George believed that in a city of three million people, the needs were great, and he openly worked with these men. An American pastor and his family serving in the southern port city of Odessa, who also had been affected by the disunity and devastation of the divisive man previously discussed, were frequent guests of the Markey family. George believed that it was vital for the pastors to come together regularly, praying for one another, for their churches, and for a further work of God in Ukraine. Tuesday mornings became a time of gathering for prayer with other local pastors. Anatoli Koluzhny, the pastor of a church called New Life, opened up his church office for prayer with other pastors and leaders from various churches. Even Orthodox priests would attend the prayer meetings as the fellowship, centered on Jesus Christ, broke through a variety of barriers. Soon, joint youth services were held at New Life, and the fellowship between churches became more and more visible. George frequently taught people in his own church, "If you meet other believers from other churches, bless them and encourage them. Don't invite them to come to our church, but encourage them to be faithful in the place where God has planted and established them."

George constantly encouraged the church to have a vision for unity in the body of Christ, and he demonstrated this by showing that he was always willing to work with others. When he was invited to teach at a Bible college or another church's Bible study, he was always open to that. When there would be interdenominational concerts or crusades, George was often at the helm directing people in the church to be involved in any way they could. Even though the young church was not officially invited to participate in a Billy Graham crusade that was taking place in Kiev, when George found out about the upcoming crusade he encouraged the body to pray and take as many people to the event as possible.

THE EXTENDING OF THE MISSION

As the work continued to grow, word began to spread about the church in Kiev. Soon, invitations began coming in from other cities for assistance in beginning churches. Dneprodzerzhinsk is a city located some 250 miles southeast of Kiev. With a population of more than 250,000 it is no small city, and, like Kiev, Dneprodzerzhinsk is a city straddling the Dnieper River. Sergey Stoma is from the left bank of Dneprodzerzhinsk. During the Soviet Union, his father had been imprisoned for his faith, Sergey himself enduring persecution for his firm belief in his Lord. One Sunday, Sergey came to the church with his son, Dima, who was studying in a university in Kiev. Dima had begun attending services at this new, young church meeting in the Zagreb movie theater, and Sergey was curious to know where his son was going. After seeing the church, and being encouraged by the passion and love of George, Sergey decided to invite George to come to his city and assist in the establishing of a church there. Sergey shares, "When I met George, I told him that we would like to open a church like this one on the left bank of our city, where there were no churches at all. But we did not know how to start, the format, or how it is done. George was immediately open to the idea, and he was on fire at the thought of coming to help open a church."

A large portion of the church prayer meetings in Kiev over the next few weeks were concerning this city and the possibilities there. Finally, it was decided that the outreaches would begin. Knowing how important it was for new believers to share their faith, George took teams of young people from the church in Kiev with him on the overnight train trips to Dneprodzerzhinsk. The trips themselves provided great opportunities for fellowship, singing, and impromptu Bible studies along the way. When the destination was reached, plans were made to show the Jesus film, and at a later date The Cross and the Switchblade, at the Mir, the only movie theater on the left bank in that city. Teams of young people from Kiev canvassed the various neighborhoods, passing out invitations. A local artist made billboards to be displayed at the theater. On the first night of the first showing, the 800-seat hall quickly filled up with more than 1,000 people, some sitting two to a seat, others standing next to the wall or sitting on balconies with feet dangling over the crowds beneath. After the film finished, people lingered, asking questions. Local band members came forward, hearts touched by the story that they had just seen.

For the next two years, George and a team from Kiev took the overnight train to Dneprodzerzhinsk on Friday nights, held church services on Saturday mornings and outreaches in the afternoons and evenings, and returned on the overnight train just in time for Sunday-morning services in Kiev. Sergey remembers, "Every Saturday, George was coming down. Back then, the trains were dirty and there were cockroaches on them. I remember George even came on the train with his wife, Pam, and their little baby. When she got up to lead worship, she gave the baby to someone to hold. And then when it was over, they went back 500 kilometers to Kiev. They had such strong convictions. For us George was an example. I remember him even holding the doors open on buses and the metro so that people could get in. He cared so much for the people, and his kids learned to do the same thing. George and the teams from the church in Kiev were the pioneers here."

In time, another American missionary came, relieving George of these trips by moving to Dneprodzerzhinsk so as to pastor this church. Sadly, this man fell into sin, and the church was painfully divided. Years later, however, Sergey recalls, "Recently, I was visiting Dneprodzerzhinsk, and I was at a service at that movie theater where it all began. About a thousand people came together from the different churches that were now on the left bank, and there were seven pastors on the stage standing together. It was an Easter celebration, and all of them had come together to celebrate the resurrection. But they were also remembering George and the foundation that had been laid there, for they all saw their roots as going back to those first years when George and the teams from Kiev came down. It was then that I understood that it had been God's will for there to be many churches in this region, not just one big one."

CHAPTER EIGHTEEN

A NEW SEASON

GEORGE REFERRED TO HIM as Mr. Eastern Europe. It was in the fall of 1990 that John Chubik first moved from the United States to Europe. Arriving in Austria, John was a part of the team of construction workers who were renovating a castle that had been purchased by Calvary Chapel of Costa Mesa to be used for a Bible college. The following years, John would be involved in missions in Bulgaria, Yugoslavia, Hungary, and Poland. While back in California at the end of 1995, and unsure of his next plans, John was called into Pastor Chuck's office. John remembers, "He had a question about a wall that had been built in Austria. And at the end of that conversation he said, 'Well, what are your plans? Where are you going to work?' I said that I wasn't sure and I was just praying about it. He then asked me, 'Have you ever thought about Russia?' I said, 'Well, no.' And he said, 'Well, there's this fellow, George Markey, who has been calling me and asking if there was anyone who could come over and help him in Kiev, Ukraine.' Pastor Chuck then gave me his phone number." However, instead of calling George, John waited. Out of the blue, that evening John received a phone call from George, who had been given John's number by Chuck Smith. "We talked for a few moments – he asked me a couple of questions and I asked him a couple of questions – and after about five minutes I just felt like, 'I could really work with this guy.' That was the thought that came into my mind. I didn't know him, but I appreciated his heart, hearing his priorities. On the basis of that conversation, I said that I would come over for one year."

After finishing some previous obligations in Poland and Hungary, John flew from Budapest to Kiev on July 1, 1996. Upon landing at the airport, John waited to meet George. He shares, "In those days, there were not many flights into Kiev, and the airport emptied out quickly. Soon no one was around and I was standing alone. I did not have any number to call George. There were no cell phones and I did not know where he lived. A police lady came over and asked me if I needed help, but there was no way to get in touch with George. So I thought if no one shows up, then I can always get on the return flight back. Finally, I looked and there was this African guy running up to me. It was Job, and he came running in, saying that they were late. George then swooped in, hugged me, and I instantly liked him. He was wearing shorts, sandals, and a Hawaiian shirt, and was tan, dynamic, and full of life. He picked up my bags as if they were nothing and we headed out to the van."

At the time of John's move to Kiev, the church was meeting in a building that we called "The Flying Saucer Building" because of its design. Sharing his first impressions of the church, John says, "Certain things surprised me. The church was relatively large, with 250 or more people. The other missionary churches that I had been a part of were generally smaller. Also, there were a lot of students, and it was interesting to see Africans there." Although there were many people coming, and a lot of activity, George was not satisfied with the spiritual life of the church. Himself having been witness to the effects of true revival in the past, George wanted the people to experience an intimacy with God that was so real that it spilled over in the form of loving actions toward the body of Christ. John remembers, "As I began to learn and look and see, I noticed that George was somewhat frustrated. Though it was clear that people were being ministered to, they had not really come to that place of ministering to each other. George told me of his desire to see people love each other more, reach out to each other more, greet one another as they came in. He was also a little frustrated with the state of the worship at that point. In the one sense there were a lot of people and excitement, but there were also things that George was wishing were at a different spiritual place."

THE MEN'S PRAYER MEETING

Some of George's frustrations seemed to be exemplified in what was taking place at the men's prayers meeting. Looking back, John says, "The meetings felt much more social than prayerful. We prayed, but usually quickly and in a 'God bless me and mine' kind of way. Seldom was their prayer for each other, and even less often for the church. Then, once prayer was over, attention moved pretty quickly to eating cookies and to having conversations about sports. It was not healthy." Never one who was afraid of stopping something that was unfruitful, or changing something that was going in the wrong direction, George made the decision to cancel the men's prayer meeting. Soon, in it's place, an all-church prayer meeting was organized and held in the church office. This new meeting would soon turn out to be a very key event in the growth of the church."

The new Monday-night prayer meeting became very central to what was happening in the church. There was noticeable growth in prayer as people began to step out of themselves and pray for others, the church, the city, and the nation. John continues, "Over time, you could hear it in people's prayers, how people began to mature and develop. The prayer meeting went from a small group to a point where it was the most happening thing in the week. We would have 50 or 60 people crammed into the office. Chairs full, couches full, people sitting in the hallway, on the floors, all the way out into the kitchen. We couldn't even fit everyone in there." Soon, that dynamic life began to flow out of the prayer meeting, and things throughout the church began to change.

Desperate to see God move, George searched to see what else was holding the church back. John remembers, "It became apparent that there were some people with fleshly attitudes, negativity, and others who had mixed motives as to why they were coming." The Wheat and the Tares. Jesus taught His disciples the parable of a man who sowed good seed into his field, but at night an enemy came and sowed tares. So, springing up from within the field were both good wheat and destructive tares, almost indiscernible in appearance until the time of harvest. Upon asking the farmer if they should remove the tares, the servants were answered, "No, lest while you gather up the tares you also uproot the wheat with them" (Matt. 13:29). The Lord Himself knew what was hindering His work in His people, and the Lord knew what needed to be done. So, instead of focusing on the removal of certain elements or individuals from the mix, George, John, and the leaders began to pray for a work of the Spirit to cleanse and strengthen the church. John continues, "We began more and more to pray for a work of the Spirit, both with the leaders and in the prayer meetings, and God began to move. Over a period of months, those with mixed motives or divided hearts either began to get right or just stopped coming. The worship and fellowship in the church began to change." God was answering prayer, and soon the atmosphere of the church was transformed. Emerging was a passion, an excitement about what God was doing, as well as an expectant hope for the future. There was a new freedom instead of fear. Boldness instead of timidity. Active love instead of passivity.

Along with this new fervency came an increased zeal for serving one another in the body, as well as in sharing their faith with others. In the fall of 1996, John and George organized a "School of Ministry" to equip people both to minister in the church and to share their faith. Evening classes were held on Tuesdays and Thursdays at a rented high school in the center of the city, including such subjects as apologetics, inductive Bible study, Old and New Testament surveys, church history, and in-depth studies of Acts, Romans, and Revelation. With an emphasis on the practical aspects of what the students were learning, frequent trips were organized to share with people on the streets of Kiev as well as outreaches to other cities. Many of those who were involved in the initial years of the School of Ministry went on to serve as pastors, missionaries, women's ministers, children's workers, and worship leaders. George loved teaching these young people, and the fruit of the school was immediate. Time and again, students would share stories in class detailing how what they had learned in the previous evening's classes had been applied in conversations at school or work the very next day. The transforming grace that had been so wonderfully received from God was being shown and taught to successive generations.

DAYS OF GRACE

David Markey remembers being a recipient of this grace from his father, and looks back at this time as a defining moment in his life. Having gone through a time when he was more rebellious toward his parents, David remembers venting his anger against his father on several occasions. Unable to fully understand what was happening with his son, George could only respond in love, by prayer, and with grace. David shares, "There was a time when I was driving Dad's car with a friend. I crashed and totaled the car. Dad came and asked if we were OK, and then dealt with the mess I had made. When we got home, I went out to the balcony of our apartment and looked out from the 15th-story window. All I could think about was how embarrassed I was, and how I wish I could just disappear. I felt like my dad would never trust me with anything ever again. I had insulted him and showed him that I was irresponsible and reckless. My mom came out and tried to calm me down. I told her I knew Dad would never entrust me with anything ever again. She responded, 'Then you don't know your father.' She told him what I said and he could not believe it. Dad came out to the balcony and put his big arm around me and said: 'David, I don't care about the car. It can be fixed. I care about you.' This act of grace changed my life and helped me understand a little better what God did for me."

THE STORY OF KRISTEN

She weighed only a few pounds and was only a few months old when they found her. Having no name, meagerly clinging to a hopeless existence, and not having any kind of future, this baby lay in the children's hospital in Kiev with a feeding tube attached to her nose and a hole in her heart. She was "broshenaya," thrown away. The unwanted child of an alcoholic mother, she was found and brought into the hospital at the same time as another baby girl. The other one died, but this one lived. She seemed to hang on.

Rhonda Markey and her friend Nicole Pratt were serving in this children's hospital as they always did, holding the babies, changing their diapers, giving them love and physical touch when no one else seemed to care. One could observe children banging their heads against their beds, or the walls, just to feel something. Why should anyone care? After all, these babies and young children were either going to die, or go back to the orphanages from which they were sent. This was the predominant opinion of the medical staff there. So what was the use?

Rhonda remembers, "The babies were not named when they first arrived, so we decided to name her. We decided on Kristen Hope. I am not sure why, but we just liked the name Kristen. The name Hope was given because of our hope that she would live. When she was nine months old, we realized that Kristen was not growing much and she didn't seem interested in her food. We asked a doctor there about her, and she said that Kristen's mom drank a lot [during pregnancy], and that Kristen had a hole in her heart which needed to be fixed with surgery. However, since she didn't have a mother to take care of her, she would not get the surgery and would eventually die." After a long period of time, Rhonda and Nicole were given permission to act as Kristen's "mothers," and they labored to get her the surgery she so desperately needed. With hearts full of hope, Nicole and Rhonda began writing people in the States about this little baby girl. They needed to raise $400 for the operation; otherwise, it would not be done. Many doctors thought why waste the resources on a hopeless, helpless, handicapped baby that would never have the opportunity of a normal life? However, friends and family in the States eagerly got involved in this need, and soon the money was raised for the surgery. Rhonda continues, "But they wouldn't do the surgery. Kristen got pneumonia and nearly died. So we had to leave her there until she was well enough for the operation." Eventually, little Kristen did recover from her pneumonia, was promised a surgery, and was given a fifty percent chance of survival after the surgery. By this time, Kristen was fourteen months old and weighed a paltry eight pounds.

"She lived through her surgery! Her name, 'Hope,' certainly fit her," shares Rhonda. "One day, the heart doctor came in to check on Kristen, and said she was getting better and could soon be discharged. The doctor said that if Kristen went back to the orphanage, she would probably die due to lack of proper care and sanitation. I asked if she thought she could come to our house to recover instead of going to the orphanage. The doctor said, 'Certainly,' and I was over the moon! I couldn't believe what I was hearing! I called Mom and told her the news! After a few days Kristen was discharged from the hospital and we took her home to our house. At last she was home."

The period of recovery went well, even though it was tiring. Having already discussed the possibility of adopting Kristen, George and Pam continued to pray about this decision. Diana Faulk remembers, "It was not an emotional decision for George and Pam, but one that they took very seriously." Furthermore, George was almost 60 years of age, and Pam already over 50. They realized that they were not as young and energetic as they used to be, and they considered the consequences of bringing a new child into their aging lives. Also, even though they were not fully aware of her fetal alcohol syndrome, they knew that she would have some difficulties that would affect her for the rest of her life. But in spite of these difficulties, George and Pam realized that there was no other hope for Kristen. They made the decision to adopt her. Diana continues, "By being with their family, Kristen would have hope, love, and a future. Otherwise, she would be lost forever if they let her go back to the orphanage." The approval for the adoption was granted in February of 1999, and Kristen received her U.S. citizenship in March of that year.

MEMORIES OF MEPHIBOSHETH

George loved to share about God's grace, using Kristen as an example: "Pity. Grace. This is how God deals with us." As George and Pam had been pitied by God and extended grace from God, so now they were facing the reality of showing this grace to another. Kristen lay in a hospital, without hope, barely existing. The family was showing her pity, extending a free gift to her that she would never be able to repay. This was not because of some goodness found in her, some potential that she may one day contribute, but because of a heart that had been touched by the grace of God—a heart of love that must act. "In this is love, not that we loved God, but that He first loved us and sent His son to be the propitiation for our sins. Beloved, if God so loved us, we also ought to love one another" (I John 4:10-11). Kristen was now rescued from an almost certain death and taken into a loving family. She was now child number nine—adopted into the family. With the adoption of Kristen began a season of international adoptions of Ukrainian orphans by American families, facilitated by the church in Kiev. Kristen's adoption also became an inspiration in the adoptions of Ukrainian orphans by Ukrainians, as they witnessed the example of grace being lavished on this little girl.

In teaching about the grace of God, George said, "Kristen was the recipient of love and pity, without any reason found within her. Just someone loved her, someone pitied her. And of course you know Kristen today. She is running around like she has never been sick a day in her life. Now she's part of a family that loves her. Why? Well, she wasn't screaming for help. She wasn't saying, 'I want a momma and a papa.' She was just dying. But you all are as Kristen. You were without hope in this world. Paul talks about it in Ephesians 2:11 and in the verses following. You were heathen, without God. One hundred percent sinful. And Jesus Christ broke down the wall that separated us from God. He removed the enmity against us, the law which condemns us. And now He says, 'Grace to you, peace!' Once you receive and know that you are saved by grace, you see that there isn't anything you can do – nothing at all - for your salvation. It was just God's pity and love—that's all. Say, 'Yes, I receive it.' That's grace. Grace is a beautiful thing. There is peace, freedom, and liberty in the grace of God."

George continued, "What about you? Has your life been touched by the grace of God? Do you understand your true condition, that your sin is actually selfishness and rebellion, separating you from a loving God? Oh, how God longs to be with you, to adopt you into His family. Do you see that you are unable to save yourself? No amount of good works can take away your sin. Truly, there exists a spiritual reality that you cannot see with your eyes, and one day you will stand before a God who pursued you for the duration of your whole life. Why do you resist? Why do you not receive the precious, life-giving sacrifice of His Son? Until the day that we pass from this life into eternity, it is never too late to admit that you are a sinner, to recognize that you cannot save yourself, and then to cry out to God, receiving Jesus as Savior and Master of your life. He will forgive you of all of your sins. God wants to change you. He loves you. He has done it all! Will you receive this wonderful grace? The Bible says, 'If you confess with your mouth the Lord Jesus and believe in your heart that God raised Him from the dead, you will be saved' (Rom. 10:9). Don't wait any longer. Begin a new life today! Open up the door of your heart to experiencing the abundant grace of God in your life."

CHAPTER NINETEEN

THE COMING STORM

THE YEARS OF 1998 and 1999, especially, would hold many trials and tragedies for both the Markeys and the ministry in Ukraine. But with the source of their strength being the grace and goodness of God, George and Pam, the family, and the church were strengthened in the Lord through these difficult times. The realities of these struggles and sufferings would yield the comfort of the Lord and the peaceable fruit of righteousness. The results of these testings and turmoils would be a deepening of their faith, a reliance on the Spirit, and the beginning of a larger move of God.

A DEADLY DIAGNOSIS

It was the fall of 1998 when George was diagnosed with prostate cancer. While on a short visit to the States, George went in for a checkup with his physician, Dr. Scott Murphy. Dr. Murphy shares, "I remember his PSA [*prostate-specific antigen*] came back at 98 when the normal was from 0 to 4. I called him and I was trying to explain to him, without making him too scared, that this was a big deal. He was at the Midwest Pastors Conference when I called him, and I said, 'George, you need to get down here and get treated.' I remember he walked through that with some sobriety, but with faith. He was very open to whatever the Lord would do, whatever the Lord would have. I really, very much thought that he would die from that. I remember when I sent him to the urologist that the urologist called me and said, 'This guy is not going to make it.' He was very dismal in his prognosis." Facing an uphill battle with cancer, George called Kiev, informing the family and team of the results of the test. Pam writes in her journal dated October 12, "Last night Dr. Scott called me and told me it was cancer, aggressive, and would need surgery."

John Chubik remembers getting the call from George. "George called me one night before the Sunday service, just after being diagnosed with cancer, saying, 'They found I have cancer, and it's looking kind of bad.' Knowing all of the implications of cancer in Ukraine, I asked, 'What do you want me to tell the church?'" With the poor state of healthcare at that time, for Ukrainians a diagnosis of cancer was basically a death sentence. Usually, cancer was never discussed, and frequently people who were diagnosed with cancer were never even told they had it. One young man in the church, Dima, had several bouts with cancer, but his family never told him that he had it. Even after having his leg amputated because of the cancer, they still never told him. As we ministered to this young man, we were strictly forbidden to tell him the truth of his condition, all the way until his death. John continues, "Knowing what a bombshell this news would be to the church, I had to ask George what I should say to the church. George said, 'Tell them. Tell them I have cancer, and tell them to pray. Tell them the Lord will see us through. I am believing God for healing, but I don't know what the Lord will do.'"

The next morning, John went to the front of the church, informing them that their pastor had cancer. "I remember standing up and making that announcement to the church," says John. "You could have heard a pin drop. They were in shock. Not only was cancer something that was not talked about publicly, but how could it happen to their pastor?" Why? Why him? Why now? The questions raced through the hearts of the people. However, as the church observed George's transparency and trust in the Lord, God would use this obstacle to increase their faith.

John continues, "There are always these natural barriers between the missionary and the people that he is coming to minister to, especially when coming from a wealthier country like America and ministering to people who are in a worse economic state. And we had heard it often. People would say, 'Well, if things get bad, you can always go back to America.' Or, 'You have this or that in America.' There was always this kind of thing that people would use to put a wall between us and them, and a reason not to believe. It was as if, somehow, maybe it was easier for us to believe the Gospel because of where we were from and what opportunities that afforded us, but not for them, in the harsher realities of their lives. When George got cancer, that was another thing that God used to bring down the walls between the missionaries and the national people. The prayer meetings were impassioned. People were praying with tears in their eyes for George to be healed. There was a love and a unity that came around that situation. And it went on for months."

As he continued to live and minister in Ukraine, George was a walking witness before the church and community of a man depending on God during the trials of life. Oleg Ignatyev shares, "When Pastor George got cancer, for me it was interesting to observe. When we found out about it, we prayed. I know they sought treatment, but he and his family did not make this sickness the most important thing to the church. He did not say things like, 'Poor us. Yes, we continue to serve, but it is so bad for us. We need a rest, we need to take a break.' No, George did not revolve the church around his sickness. Often it seems that when preachers become burdened with a problem, or perhaps there is sickness, lack of work, or struggle in their lives or families, then they start to complain, saying, 'Oh, this is a difficult time, I want to take a break, gather my thoughts, let someone else preach for a while.' No, from George I never heard that. I know that it must have been very difficult for George and the family, but it didn't negatively affect the church. For me, that was an example. He remembered what was the most important. He continued to live as an example. I know that George and the family had a lot of problems, but he knew how to rejoice in all things, and he transmitted that to the people."

Pastors and churches around the world began to hear of George's cancer, and they began to pray. Due to the potential problems associated with surgery, George began looking into other options for treatment. Hearing of a facility in Washington state that was performing experimental radioactive seed implants, George checked with Dr. Murphy to see whether he thought it would be a good option for him. "He said, 'Hey what do you think if I do this?'" shares Dr. Murphy. "At that point I thought, 'Whatever you want to try is fine, because the overall hope is not great anyway.' George seemed to understand, medically, how serious this was. Yet he just kind of walked through it step by step, one thing at a time. And one test after another, just kept coming up negative. It hadn't spread and lo and behold—You know, as a doctor, I hear these stories of 'So and so was healed.' As a doctor, maybe I am more cynically minded, but there are very, very few people where I feel like, that person was absolutely, without question, healed. But when I think of George's prostate cancer, I can say that I believe, without question, he was healed. His cancer is probably the most glaring example that I have ever seen of a person being healed."

THE END OF THE ROAD?

It would be just a few short months after George's diagnosis that another test came upon the church in Kiev. Having arrived in Ukraine at a time when the economy was in a state of ruin, and with the majority of this new church being young people, George had always chosen to supply the funds for the rent of the church's meeting place. However, in January of 1999 there came a time when George's support from the States had dwindled to the point that he was no longer able to pay the rent. John shares, "Even though we had 250 people, the offerings were like five or seven dollars, which was nothing, even for Ukrainians. Through this you could see that the people hadn't taken ownership. They were happy to come, and they were being ministered to by the Word and the love of George and Pam and the fellowship. They were happy to receive at that point, but it was not wholly theirs yet. As the prayer meeting was going on, as the Holy Spirit was doing His work in taking away certain elements, eventually this night came when George was just trusting the Lord for the rent money for the hall there, but it didn't come. They got their monthly statements and there were no funds to pay for the rent of the hall. George just said, 'This will be our last Sunday. Tomorrow is our last Sunday. So what are we going to do?' The only thing we could do was to break up into home groups. We figured out all of these places where we could have meetings and who would be teaching, perhaps eight or more home groups. We thought that we will just put out these little milk cartons at each study, and people can put money into these milk boxes, and we will collect it until we have enough to pay for two months' rent."

John continues, "We met for a couple of months in the home groups. At the end of that time, we counted the money that had come in, and we had enough money for two months' rent. From that time forward, no missionaries ever had to give any money to pay for the church's rent. The people took financial ownership of the church through that. It was a huge step forward. It was something that happened almost against George's will. He was so gracious and so generous that if he would have had the funds, he would have paid the rent for sure. But God just brought him to a place where financially he couldn't do it, and that opened the door for the Lord to allow the Ukrainians to step forward and take ownership in that way."

THE FILLING OF THE HOLY SPIRIT

After making a brief trip to Poland for the finalizing of Kristen's adoption, and then to the States for the cancer treatment, George, Pam, and newly adopted Kristen returned to Ukraine in May of 1999. Upon his return, it was George's desire to have a church retreat in the fall. George not only had been teaching about the need for the filling of the Holy Spirit, and praying for a work of the Spirit, but also wanted to provide an opportunity for the people of the church to gather for an extended time of worship and simply waiting on God to do anything He wanted to do.

In the month of September of 1999, Calvary Chapel of Kiev held its first church retreat at a small conference center on the outskirts of the city. Pastor Bill Goodrich was one of the main speakers at this event, as well as George, John Chubik, and other missionaries who had arrived to serve in Ukraine. With the plan of going through the Book of Ephesians, the emphasis of the main session was on the work of the Holy Spirit. John remembers, "On Saturday evening there was a very simple teaching, and then there was an altar call. The question was asked, 'Does anyone want to receive this power of the Holy Spirit to be a witness?' And then it just happened. As people opened their hearts to Him, the Lord lovingly poured out His Holy Spirit. People were coming forward saying, 'We want the baptism of the Holy Spirit. We want to serve Jesus.' They were broken and weeping. When it was all over, Bill, George, and George Robert were standing around rejoicing in what God had done. George said, 'This is it. It's all different now.' This was a watershed moment in the history of the church. It was God's timing. That for which George had been believing and praying had come to pass. George had known such a thing could happen because he had seen it during the time of the Asbury revival. He knew what a work of the Holy spirit could do and he was seeking it for the believers in Ukraine. A lot of us had never seen anything like that, how God could change a group of people in a night. But we saw it that night."

The change in the church was dramatic. After years of sowing, tending, and cultivating, the seed that had fallen on good ground, now watered by the Holy Spirit, had matured and began yielding the fruit of the Spirit. Love became the dominant force in the church: a longing for fellowship, compassion toward those going through suffering, and the desire to see people come to know Jesus. In a teaching that he shared at a conference in Hungary, George said, "For many years there in Kiev we were evangelizing, trying to do a work of the Lord. But we had never really given time or a place for people to receive the filling of the Holy Spirit. We rented facilities where you had to get out quickly when it was over. I will never forget the last night of that conference. The Holy Spirit descended upon that place. We didn't make it happen. And I can tell you, the church has never been the same since. From that point on, everything changed. The worship was dynamic. Because when people are baptized with the Holy Spirit, there is a greater passion for worship. And from that point on, God prepared us for the planting of churches. The Lord has allowed us now to be involved in the planting of nine churches, most of them after that moment. In one of his last messages, George shared, "There would be no Book of Acts without the baptism of the Holy Spirit, and there would be no good work in Ukraine without the baptism of the Holy Spirit. Only after that time were other churches planted in Ukraine, for a person who is not filled with the Holy Spirit cannot effectively minister to the spirit of man."

THE MULTIPLICATION OF THE MODEL

It finally began to happen. Other pastors were now coming from the States, desiring to be a part of what God was doing in Ukraine. As they arrived in Ukraine, George would encourage them to stay in Kiev for a period of time to observe the church, get to know the people, and prayerfully consider where God would have them serve. After six months or a year, these pastors would then venture out into other cities in Ukraine, taking groups of people from the church in Kiev to assist them in the establishing of new churches. Large cities like Poltava, Dnepropetrovsk, Zaporozhia, and Kharkiv, and smaller cities like Preluki, Chernigiv, and Kagarlik. Some of those Ukrainians who went out on these trips would end up staying for years as missionaries to their own people in these other cities. Sasha Andreashina, who continues to travel to other cities in Ukraine, shares, "George always respected Ukrainians. He always wanted to see us ministering to our own people. In fact, a big percent of my love for my country was influenced by George."

The following spring, May of 2000, was the first national conference of Calvary Chapel churches in Ukraine. Not limited to Ukraine, the conference drew pastors and leaders from churches in the neighboring countries of Moldova and Poland as well. Missionaries who were serving in Austria and Hungary also arrived, assisting with the teaching and enjoying being a part of what God was doing among these Ukrainian churches. Over the course of the next few years, upwards of 800 to 900 people would come annually to these conferences from all over Ukraine and the world. Remembering the national conference in 2006, Pastor David Guzik shares, "In coming for the national conference, Inga-Lill and I were both deeply impressed at both the love and the maturity among the Ukrainian believers and leadership. It spoke to me about how effectively God had used George and others to make disciples and build effective churches in Ukraine. Plus, there was simply a lot of joy and fun at the conference." The impact from these conferences touched not only Ukrainians, but George's family as well.

A CHANGED LIFE

Jon Markey had just turned 14 and was very involved with competitive soccer. Having played for years, even internationally, Jon had finally come to a point where he was the starting goalie for the team. He was being encouraged by his coach that if he stuck with the game he could really "make it big." With the goal of being a professional soccer player at the forefront of his life, Jon was upset when his mother informed him that he would be going to the church retreat that fall, no questions asked. Jon shares, "There was a really big game coming up for us in the fall, and I had worked my way to be the starting goalie. There was a lot of competition there." For Jon not to make that game, he was risking the possibility of others taking his place as starting goalie. Jon continues, "But I remember Mom just determining that I was not going to miss the conference, and I knew that Mom was as stubborn as me, and she was not going to back down. She really wanted me to be there, and I was really upset about it, put out because I knew what it was going to mean for me to miss the game."

Obediently, but not happily, Jon went to the conference. He continues, "Up to that point I had been really hesitant to say anything about my faith. So explaining to the coach why I wasn't going to make it to the game, or to any of the players, was hard because I didn't want to just say that the reason was because of church. So I went to the conference, and pretty much immediately the Lord started working in my heart. He was trying to say something, trying to really get ahold of me. The theme of the conference was Philippians 1:21, 'For me to live is Christ.' I think Bill Goodrich was doing most of the teaching at the conference and sharing, but the thing is, it wasn't what anyone actually said, but it was just that verse in Philippians by itself. It was the Holy Spirit using the Word of God. It was the worship."

Jon continues, "There were times where the worship was going on and people were praying. I remember, I didn't know exactly what I was looking for, but I knew I needed to get prayer and I needed to pray. I remember going up to Bill Goodrich, and I remember he prayed for me to be filled with the Spirit. Though I don't remember a moment when that happened, I just remember that it consumed me, the work of the Holy Spirit in my heart. It was all I wanted to think. All I wanted to do was worship and praise God, glorifying Him with everything. Through it all, the fruit was just that I wanted to give my life to Christ completely. I believed in the Lord, but I hadn't surrendered my life fully to Him. I was doing many things in the flesh and living for myself. That was the point at which I did a 180 and committed my life to Christ and everything that I do. And so that changed soccer. It changed where I wanted to go, what I wanted to do with my life. Soccer became very unimportant. I told my mom that I really believed the Lord wanted me to use my gifts at music to the best of my ability. So I went to music college. And again, that all happened at the same time. I still had a lot of problems and things to work through, I still do, but that was when the Lord got ahold of my life. And even through all the problems, the bottom line is that my desire is to follow the Lord, and not simply to have the Lord help me with my plans."

Amazed at the changes taking place in his son, George frequently shared with others about this dynamic transformation. Dr. Scott Murphy recalls, "The biggest memory that I have of George is this, and I can remember the exact table where we were sitting when he told me. This still chokes me up. Everybody always talked about the church in Kiev and how the church was changed. Bill would come home and say, 'It's like the church in the Book of Acts over there.' But do you know what George's report on it was? He said, 'You should see my son Jon.' I love that, that George definitely had a heart for ministry, but I think the biggest deal of that whole thing for George was that Jonny was no longer interested in soccer. He was now interested in the Lord. It seems like I heard George say it half a dozen times, 'You should see my son Jon.' He was just so touched by that. George was as hard-core and passionate about the church as anyone, but it always struck me to see his excitement over the changes in his son."

WORSHIP AND WITNESSING

It was about this same time when the Lord began doing a new work in a different region of the city. In Traeshina, another very populated part of Kiev, so many young people were getting saved in this part of the city that many evenings of the week were filled with Bible studies and outreaches there. George Robert and John Chubik would frequently lead these studies or outreaches to that community. Among these new young people were gifted musicians, poets, linguists, and even athletes. As they were filled with the Holy Spirit, the result was not only a desire to reach out to those who did not know Jesus, but also an overflow in hearts full of praise to God. There was a new inspiration for writing songs bringing glory to God.

The church's first worship album, Bread of Life, was released in 2001. It was one of the first Ukrainian worship albums in the country, and was full of fresh new songs. Received well by other churches in Ukraine, the worship team was soon being invited to play at coffeehouses, conferences, and other churches. John Chubik shares, "It was like musicians were coming out of the woodwork, and they were highly trained and very skilled. All of a sudden we had three and four worship teams, and we could send musicians out all over the place. I thought back to those prayer meetings when George was praying, 'Lord, bless the worship team,' when there was no worship team. He had such great faith, speaking of those things as though they were, when they weren't."

AWESOME OPPORTUNITIES

One of the first large outreach opportunities that the church was able to participate in was a crusade involving David Wilkerson. As the life and ministry of David Wilkerson had been so instrumental in George's life, it was an honor and a privilege to be a part of this interdenominational crusade in Kiev. Our church was responsible for a portion of the worship, as well as the follow-up after this event. The evening before the crusade was a special dinner in which George was able to meet David Wilkerson, sharing with him about the influence that he had been in his life and ministry both in the States and in Ukraine. As 5,000 people filled the Sports Palace, the worship team led out in "Bread of Life" and other songs from their album. Hearts were touched, and after the message, dozens of workers from our church began ministering to the people who were coming forward.

Other ministry opportunities, such as the Ukrainian "Mi Chas" (My Time) Christian music festival and the international "Passion" worship conferences, began involving people from the church. Soon, these youth and worship festivals were becoming an annual event. Once again, the worship team was frequently invited to participate and lead in these large events, involving many different churches, many organizations, and thousands of young people. George's teachings and examples of working with other churches in supporting and promoting the unity of the body were being reproduced.

WEDDINGS AND BABIES

Since the church was mostly made up of young people who were serving together, it naturally followed that in time they would become interested in each other. Soon it seemed that weddings were taking place monthly, and sometimes every week. An entire generation of believing families was coming into being, and with that came the children. As George and Pam counseled these many different couples before they were married, they also spoke wisdom into their lives in how to raise children.

George loved weddings. For him it was one of the greatest times of celebration. Years earlier, in 1994, he had officiated my marriage to his eldest daughter, Renee. It was the first wedding in the church in Kiev, attended by over 200 people and performed in a palace in the center of Kiev. People were amazed to witness the Western-style wedding complete with worship led by the family, George preaching the Gospel, and a reception with a live Christian band. George was always extra radiant and joyful at weddings, excited to be involved in the beginning of a new family as well as to be given the opportunity to share the Gospel with mostly unbelieving family members.

George knew the importance of these marital relationships. They were living examples of the relationship between Christ and the church. There was potential that these marriages would be a tremendous blessing and even a witness for the Lord, but if built on a wrong foundation, they could hinder a person's walk with the Lord, their effectiveness as ministers of the Gospel, or even the church. In writing his letters to Timothy and Titus, the Apostle Paul emphasized the importance of the family, how the husband treats his wife, and how he leads his children. In writing to the Corinthians, Paul wrote of the importance of marrying a believer. In George's last message that he shared in Crawfordsville before moving to Ukraine, he spoke about the race that we are running, and of those things that can hinder us in this race, one of those things being our own children. For this reason, George had Pam share with the congregation biblical principles on raising children. It was his vision to see families grow and prosper in the Lord, thus being a testimony to others of the love of God.

Whatever resources could be used to further someone's walk with Jesus, George made the attempt to share them, whether books, or inviting special speakers to teach, or opening their own home for people to come over at any moment. The people of the church knew that George loved them so much that he wanted to do everything possible for them to succeed. It seemed that these new families were getting together, praying, and sharing with one another all of the time. Whether these events were couples' retreats, men's and women's retreats, special dinners, or celebrations, these extended times of fellowship in the Word were producing lasting fruit. To this day, I have a hard time thinking of a single married couple from that time in the church who is not still together, and many are serving in ministry together.

CAMPING TRIPS

The summer weather afforded George the opportunity of taking the youth on frequent camping trips. Having brought back 50 sleeping bags with him from an earlier trip to Holland, George would pack as many guys in the van as he could fit, sometimes making multiple trips if necessary, and head out of town for times of swimming, campfires, and nights under the stars. These were times that united the hearts of these young men with each other and with God. For George it was all about investing himself in others. His time, resources, knowledge, and experience were invaluable to these who were seeking to grow in life and their relationship with the Lord.

CHAPTER TWENTY

TURNING THE WORK OVER, MOVING ON

It CAME AT A TIME when everyone was away. Pam was gone, assisting in the birth of a grandchild in the States. John Chubik and his wife of seven years, Karen, were on furlough in the States, visiting family and churches. Even George Robert and his wife of three years, Sharon, were away in France, getting new visas for Ukraine. It happened on a Sunday in February of 2006. George finished preaching the sermon and came to the back of the hall to greet people, as he usually did. Only this time it was different. As I locked eyes with George after the service, the words came out of my mouth before I even realized it. "It's time to go, isn't it," I said. "Yes, it's time to go," was George's reply. And with that simple, brief conversation both of us knew that somewhere an invisible timer began, counting down the days to the end of 14 years of ministry in Kiev.

Not even wanting to fellowship with anyone after the service, we raced home and began openly sharing about all that was on our hearts. Unsettled. Conversations between George and me were long and intense, and led to times of prayer. There was a period of an uneasy restlessness, and a desire to be sensitive to anything the Holy Spirit might be saying. New direction. Although there was a certain stability in the church in that leaders were being raised up, missionaries were being sent out, and other churches were being started, the time had come to deal with the remaining physical presence of the foreign missionary leadership in the church in

Kiev. Confirmation. As we continued to talk and pray, it became obvious that something similar was on our hearts. "Jed and I have been talking," George told Bill Goodrich as he spoke with him by phone. Remembering the period leading up to this decision, Bill shares, "George had been saying, 'I feel like I am not doing anything.'" Even though he was as busy as ever, much of the work of the ministry had been delegated to Ukrainians. John Chubik shares, "I remember very clearly coming back after I had been in the States, and we just sat down and talked—George was saying things like, 'I think we're done,' and, 'I don't wanna stay too long,' and, 'I recognize that I can hinder the work.' I then understood that the pillar of fire was beginning to move."

It did not happen in the way that one would expect it to happen. Logically, it would make more sense to have a pastor in the process of taking over the work before the current pastor would leave. Strategically, it would make more sense to have someone to whom the administrative work of the ministry could be turned over before the change was announced. All that we had was the calling – an unsettledness, a new direction, and a confirmation – but that was enough. So, by faith, we decided to make the announcement to the church body of that which the Lord had put on our hearts. That Monday-evening prayer meeting and the following Wednesday-night announcement to a larger group from the church were some of the saddest, most challenging times. In a newsletter, I wrote the following: "I couldn't pray. I could only sing. The night we announced to the church body that the Lord was moving us on was a much anticipated, yet difficult evening. Afterward, I could not speak with people without tears welling up in my eyes."

On March 7, 2006, the following joint newsletter was sent out by our families: "The time has come to give full responsibility for Calvary Chapel of Kiev to national leadership. Tonight at a corporate prayer meeting, we announced our intentions to the church to move on. Now the question is, where do we go from here? ... Other cities in Ukraine? Other countries? ... When we first came to Kiev in July of 1992, we had a vision to plant a church, hand it over to the nationals, and move on to plant other churches in the former Soviet Union. Since then we have been privileged to watch God surpass our expectations. In the last nearly fourteen years, not only have we seen a strong church established in Kiev, but we have seen eleven daughter and granddaughter churches planted in different cities around Ukraine. ... We have been able to ordain Ukrainian pastors, and we have a church board that consistently makes sound spiritual decisions. Besides that, the church is now operationally independent of our financial support."

NATIONAL LEADERS

George had already begun asking some of the Ukrainian leaders if they felt that it was time for there to be a Ukrainian pastor. These discussions often ended on a note of hesitation by the Ukrainians, unsure of whether they could perform the task, and uncertain whether they wanted the responsibility. With ordained elders already serving in the church, conversations began with one of the elders, Alosha Satenko, about the possibility of his taking over the pastorate.

Alosha, ordained by George and other pastors, had been sent out from the church in Kiev and was serving as pastor in a newly planted church in the nearby village of Borodyanka. Alosha and his wife, Yulia, had come from a hard background, but were living examples of lives changed and filled by the Spirit. Alosha shares, "I grew up without a father. George was like a father to me." Having worked in children's ministry in the church in Kiev, taught Bible studies, and served in various outreaches, Alosha had seen many aspects of church life and ministry. Himself employed as a driver for the metro, Alosha was an example of a person who was not afraid of work, and was obviously not in the ministry for the money. After much prayer, it was decided that Alosha would begin teaching the Sunday services, assisted by some of the other men as well.

THE DECISION

At first, not sensing a release from Ukraine, we continued praying about and pursing opportunities in other cities in Ukraine. Places like Donetsk, which George had traveled to earlier and where he desired to see a church planted; Nickolaev, which a young couple from the church in Kiev had recently moved to; and Lugansk, in the far eastern part of Ukraine – all were cities that became the object of more intense prayer. One by one, however, the doors began to close to those places. At the same time, an invitation was forthcoming from a different country.

Paul and Melanie (Markey) Billings had recently married, and even more recently had moved to Bishkek, Kyrgyzstan. A small country of five million people, situated in the mountains west of China, Kyrgyzstan is a nation with a population that is approximately 80 percent Muslim. In November of 2005, taking the five-day train ride through Russia and Kazakhstan, Paul and Melanie arrived in Bishkek and began praying about the beginning of a church. On a day in late February of 2006, after hearing of the recent decision in Kiev, Paul and Melanie called the family in Kiev, inviting them to come and help in the establishing of a new church there. Still unsure of where to go, George and Pam made the decision to take a trip to Bishkek to assist with the birth of Paul and Melanie's first child, as well as to pray about the possibility of moving there.

George and Pam's visit to Bishkek was a refreshing time for Paul and Melanie, and it was also a time of increased vision for Paul. "For the first two months when we were there, we visited many different churches in Bishkek," shares Paul. "Through that time we understood that none of the churches were teaching systematically through the Bible—it was all topical. When we were invited to come to Kyrgyzstan by Pastor Sasha Kim, he told us that there was a huge need for good churches there." Little by little, Paul and Melanie began making relationships with those people around them. Soon, Paul began teaching a small home Bible study in their apartment with these new friends. Paul shares, "When George came that spring, we had a couple of people coming to our apartment for a Bible study—that was all. But George's vision was so big. He said things like, 'You need to find a place in the center of the city.' I said, 'But George, we only have two people coming and don't have any money to pay for the rent of a place in the center.'" Seemingly unfazed by any of those logical arguments, George led Paul to the center of the city and began looking around.

A CHURCH AT THE METRO PUB

Located right next to the office of the Mayor and on the most central street in Bishkek is a restaurant called the Metro Pub. In what was formerly a puppet theater during Soviet times, the Metro Pub serves a clientele mainly composed of those from the expatriate community. The facility is divided into two sections. As one walks into the building, the restaurant is located in the front-most section. At the back of the restaurant are closed doors that lead into what used to be the puppet theater. With a hall that could easily seat up to 300 people, this part of the building had fallen into disrepair, and was mainly used for the occasional concert, wedding reception, dance party, or even boxing match. As George began talking with the manager, a rough-talking, middle-aged Englishman, he inquired as to the availability of the large back hall of the restaurant for use on Sundays. Since the restaurant did not open until later in the day, especially on Sundays, George was told that it was available. Upon hearing that George and Paul were interested in having church services there, the manager said that they could use it free. God had provided a place where the young congregation would meet for the next year.

In Kyrgyzstan, in order to teach publicly on religious matters, all foreigners are required to obtain a special certificate of permission for religious activity granted by the governmental agency of religious affairs. Sitting down with the official in this governmental office, Paul explained who he was and what had been done in Ukraine. Paul remembers, "The man told me, 'We know that the majority of foreign missionaries working here are doing so underground, secretly, and we know who they are. But since you have been open with me, I can tell you that it will go better for you.'" Over the next three months, Paul waited for his religious permission, sometimes coming into the office daily to remind them by his presence. Perhaps it took so long because they were waiting for a bribe, but eventually he received the official permission from the office.

Within a couple of weeks, a team of Ukrainians from Kiev arrived in order to help with the beginning of a new church in Bishkek. Having already been informed by almost every missionary there of the impossibilities of doing open evangelism on the streets, let alone for a foreigner to start a church, they shared much concern that any overt attempts at outreach would be quickly extinguished by the authorities. However, after much prayer, plans were made for a week of daily outreaches involving dramas, music, and gospel presentations. Crowds formed around the teams as they performed, at times swelling up to a couple hundred observers. It was interesting to watch the crowds during the dramatic portrayal of Jesus' crucifixion, as perhaps 30 percent of them would leave, unable to believe that God the Savior came, died, and rose again. Leaflets were handed out and posters hung, inviting people to a weekend showing of the blockbuster movie The Passion of Christ at the Metro Pub. Only one time did a police officer approach Paul and the team, asking about what they were doing and requesting to see Paul's religious permission.

It was beginning all over again. That which had been done from small towns in Kentucky to metropolitan cities in Ukraine was now beginning again in the far-away country of Kyrgyzstan. It was the living of a godly example and the establishing of a model church, based on the systematic teaching of the Word of God and the reliance on the Holy Spirit, with the goal of equipping the believers for the work of the ministry.

Returning to Kiev, George and Pam were excited about what was taking place in Bishkek, yet the big question remained. Was the Lord calling them to Kyrgyzstan? So far, it had seemed that the Lord had been closing the doors to other cities in Ukraine. But in Kyrgyzstan, there were obvious needs, invitations, and a ready team of family to join with in the ministry. So, at 64 years of age, and in view of these needs and invitations to Kyrgyzstan, George stepped through the open door, resolved in his heart that the Lord was calling them further east. Another season of life and ministry was beginning for the Markeys—only this time in Central Asia.

The decision to move to Bishkek was made on June 1, 2006, and as the Lord had called me to serve alongside George for the previous 14 years, so I believed that God would have us continue together. The church in Kiev was behind us, sending us out as their missionaries to further the Gospel. Both of our families packed our belongings into a container, sent it ahead of us by train, and flew to Bishkek on July 26, 2006. The night before we left Kiev, instead of the usual Monday-night prayer meeting, a baptism was held at the Dnieper River. The model was continuing, even in the departure — ministering to new believers, showing the importance of reaching out. After the baptisms, in the glow of the evening sunlight, the laughter and rejoicing turned into times of prayer and goodbyes on the sandy stretch of beach.

SILK ROAD AWAKENING

As the rising morning sun washed over the mountainous peaks surrounding the city of Bishkek, the nearby Islamic calls to prayer rang throughout the city. Coming from Kiev, which seems to have only 60 days of sunshine a year, the promise of 300 days of sunshine a year in Kyrgyzstan was a warm welcome indeed. For 14 years the Markeys had been living in cramped apartments, sometimes even separating the family into multiple apartments when large enough ones could not be found. Now they had moved into a house on the outskirts of Bishkek. This house was located in the middle of a Kyrgyz community, the protruding minaret of the nearest mosque visible from the upstairs window.

Kyrgyzstan is a mixture of cultures, traditions, and peoples. Whether Kyrgyz, Russian, Uzbek, Uighur, Dungan, or one of the many other nationalities, the various people groups who populate Central Asia are well known for their hospitality. For them, relationships are prized over money. It is easy, even required, to meet and get to know your neighbors. In this country whose people are family oriented and have a great esteem for elders, George, Pam, and their two remaining at-home kids, Aaron and Kristen, were warmly welcomed and shown great respect.

RENEWAL CHURCH

Sunday mornings in Bishkek began by picking up cigarette butts and beer bottles that were scattered around the hall from the night before. Chairs, lights, sound, and music equipment were then set up for the Sunday-morning service. Behind the stage, rooms were readied for the Sunday school classes and youth group. Special attention had to be made to the gaping hole in the corner of the floor so that no child or teacher would step into it and collapse the floor.

With his first message taken from the Gospel of John, chapter 10, George spoke about Jesus. "Jesus is the door; He is the good shepherd." In a country known for raising sheep, George shared his own sheep-raising stories, the importance of knowing the voice of the shepherd, and His promise to take care of His sheep. A former Muslim woman from Tajikistan came up after the service and shared with us about her conversion to Christianity. "I had a dream...," and beginning with her testimony, we soon began to hear many share of the frequency of God speaking to Muslims through dreams and visions. God was doing a special work across the Muslim world.

In the beginning, those who were coming were mostly new believers, but we were soon joined by many missionaries who had been kicked out of the neighboring country of Uzbekistan. This "crack-down on Western imperialism" was, in fact, a retaliation against the West for making an issue of the Andijan massacre – a dark day in May of 2005 when government forces slaughtered hundreds, if not thousands, of demonstrators, disposing of their unidentified bodies in mass graves.

In successive weeks, George began teaching through the Book of Acts. He coherently laid out a foundational understanding of Jesus, and His death, burial, resurrection, and ascension, as well as spending much time on the work of the Holy Spirit. Although I had been listening to George teach for the previous 20 years, I had never heard him teach the Book of Acts so passionately and effectively. In the months that followed, mid-week Bible studies and a school of ministry were also begun.

Pasha Bolshakov was one of the first young people to begin attending the church. Pasha shares, "I remember when Pastor George came, and the first time I saw him – he was really happy. He was always smiling and shaking everyone's hands. He was preaching that day, and I just realized it was the simplicity of the Word that was so beautiful. There was nothing man-made. He was always open to talk to people, especially with the young guys who came. He was always there to answer the questions, always smiling. I remember one time they invited us to their house for Christmas dinner. They were living way outside of Bishkek. It was just really simple, nothing artificial. It was like, 'Hey, here we are. Come join us.'"

NOMADS

Central Asia is known for its nomads. Historically, wandering clans would roam the vast mountain ranges with their sheep, coming down into the valleys in order to buy, sell, and trade as needed. The nomadic Kyrgyz people, in particular, were more shielded from centuries of forced Islamization due to the fact that Islam took root mostly in cities, and not the countryside. To this day, perhaps as a result of their nomadic past, the Muslims of Kyrgyzstan, especially in the northern part of the country, practice a more mixed and nominal Islam than in other parts of the Muslim world. However, this is rapidly changing with each passing year as the youth are more and more radicalized.

The youth are the future of any country, and George's desire to reach the young people never changed, no matter how old he was. In seeking to use any and all means possible to meet and share with people, evenings of English movies at the Metro Pub turned into the founding of a youth center, which we called Nomads. With up to one hundred kids coming for our special events, Nomads became a point of contact with the youth. With ping-pong tables, board games, English lessons, movies, music, tea, food, and lots of couches and chairs, Nomads was everything from an after-school hangout to a conversational English school with classes multiple times a week. It was interesting to hear George teach English at Nomads, complete with his own country/hick, Hoosier pronunciations of certain words and phrases. However, at our Christmas party in December of 2006, the students wanted to get their picture taken with George in particular.

"SECRETARY OF STATE"

Standing outside of the downtown mall, Beta Stores, George was always interested in meeting people. What better way than to act like the lost foreigner that he was? Examining his map in view of the wealthy man seated nearby in the expensive black Mercedes, George began asking directions in broken Russian and incomplete English. Getting out of his car, the man answered in good English, to the surprise of George. However, every attempt of George to lay his map on the hood of the Mercedes was met with resistance by the English-speaking Kyrgyz gentlemen. The man was surprised that George was actually "living" in Bishkek and not just a tourist, and the conversation turned to the matter of why George would give up living in America for a life in Kyrgyzstan. He was not a businessman, not a tourist. George was able to share the hope of Jesus Christ with this man, and only later saw from his business card that he held a position in the government of Kyrgyzstan equivalent to our Secretary of State.

ROADWORK

One of the last memories I have of George before he got sick has to do with his determination to do something about the roads near his house. While driving in Kyrgyzstan, one must be extra vigilant so as to dodge the ever-widening, ever-deepening potholes. In George's mind, what better way to be a witness to those of his neighbors who had vehicles than to help fix the roads? When George was able to find pieces of broken asphalt around the city, he would load them into his car, drive them back, and begin patching the holes in the roads leading to his community. Except for those people who were driving past with dumbfounded expressions on their faces, most drivers would frequently pass by nodding in approval of what he was doing, or even stopping to try to speak with him. The last hole that I remember George fixing was directly in front of the mosque near his house.

THE CALVARY CHAPEL MISSIONS CONFERENCE

From the moment I snapped his picture for the brochure, George had been excited to share at the upcoming Calvary Chapel Missions Conference in southern California. What was he going to share before these 900 people? What could be of use for the missionaries who would attend, as well as for those who were considering going to the mission field? The answer: his life. As with any of us, our lives are made up of a collection of failures, successes, hurts, dreams, frustrations, and victories. Typically, we love the positive, and move the negative into the basement of our brokenness. In reality, though, it is God who works all things together for good to those who love Him (Rom. 8:28). Within that mess called life are some amazing stories, helpful examples, and significant warnings that are woven together by a sovereign God to use as He best determines.

George's life is what you will hear if you listen to his teaching from that conference. And it is his life that remains an example for all of us of what God can do with a man who is yielded to Him. George spoke of three things: the call of God, the preparation of His servant, and the work. Expounding on these three points, George painted an interesting picture of his own humanness with stories from his own life and experiences, but even more so, he revealed the greatness of a God who works in spite of us. At the end of his message, culminating in the finishing of the work in Ukraine, George asks the question, "How did we know it was time to leave?" He answers, "God laid it upon my heart. The Lord showed us the same things." Citing Jesus' message to the disciples, George shared with the congregation what he had previously spoken to the church in Kiev before his departure. "Most assuredly, I say to you, he who believes in Me, the works that I do he will do also; and greater works than these he will do, because I go to My Father. And whatever you ask in My name, that I will do, that the Father may be glorified in the Son. If you ask anything in My name, I will do it." (John 14:12-14)

Greater works, greater things. George expected God to do much more through the church in Kiev after his departure, if they would remain in unity and rely on the power of the Spirit. Never one to be satisfied with the present, George concluded his message with a call to further work, a challenge for people to see the need in the surrounding Central Asian republics. His vision was for beyond the now, pressing into the future. The needs are so obvious. The possibilities are so immense. The God of the harvest is so generous, but the laborers are so few. And so we wait for more pastors, leaders, and workers to see the need to step into the distant fields of world missions. Could it be that God has a work for you?

CHAPTER TWENTY ONE

THE FINAL DEPARTURE

GEORGE MADE IT BACK to Bishkek from the States on January 19, 2007, just in time for Aaron's 15th birthday. Since the family routinely did not manage to celebrate birthdays on the actual day, Aaron was excited that he was able to go out to eat with his dad that day, just the two of them. Our youngest daughter, Rachel, had been born just a couple of weeks before, while George was in the States. I can still see him sitting in the chair in our home tenderly grasping her in his big arms, the last grandchild that he would ever hold. In seemingly good health, George laughed, saying that he had just applied for Social Security. He had even gotten a pair of dumbbells and was exercising, looking forward to Pam returning from her trip to Ukraine. Things were good.

On Friday, January 26, George woke up violently ill. At first thinking it was the flu, Melanie and Renee began treating him for that. However, it soon became apparent that this was no ordinary flu. When we contacted an American doctor in Bishkek and explained to him George's condition, he immediately informed us that George needed to go to the hospital, thinking that it could be appendicitis or worse. Paul and Melanie attempted to make George as comfortable as possible in the car and began the drive to the hospital. As they neared the hospital, the road seemed to run out, as the bumps and holes were inescapable. With every jolt and roll George let out a torturous moan or cry. Whatever he was sick with was more serious than anyone had imagined.

After they managed to walk up to the second floor of the hospital, Paul talked with the main surgeon, informing him of George's condition. The doctor decided on immediate surgery and George was promptly wheeled away. However, as the two-hour-long procedure turned into four hours, it became obvious that what was going on was more than an appendectomy. Peering through the operating window, Paul and Melanie observed that many other doctors were gathering, intently studying the operation. Someone was even filming the procedure. A nurse suddenly appeared from behind the doors motioning Paul into the corridor. She then explained that George's condition was very serious, and that the problem was not with his appendix, but with his pancreas. The diagnosis, pancreatic necrosis. The main surgeon later would explain that, throughout the world, 80 to 90 percent of people with this condition die. As the nurse spouted out a long list of medicines that were needed immediately in order to begin treating George, Paul and I quickly wrote down the names and began going from pharmacy to pharmacy looking for them.

The medical situation in many eastern-European and post-Soviet nations is much different than in the West. In the West we have a culture where the hospital seeks to provide the best treatment, medicines, and care possible to the patient, the physical burdens associated with such care being absorbed by the hospital staff. In other countries, the level of care received by the patient is dependent on the resources and connections of the patient. Family is critical at this time. For example, most medicines are not maintained and provided by the hospital, but must be located, purchased, and sometimes even administered by the family. Furthermore, any medicines that are purchased for the patient need to be closely monitored since it is very common for the underpaid hospital staff or other patients to "borrow" some for themselves. If you are sick and in the hospital in the former Soviet Union, you need to be very proactive about your treatment or have an advocate to basically fight for good treatment on your behalf. For this and other reasons, we soon realized that it is best not to have to go to the hospital if at all possible. It is true that things are changing, but as with most reforms in the former Soviet Union, they are changing very slowly.

As a foreigner, George was given the best treatment possible. After the operation and a short period in intensive care, George was released to his own private room, and we were permitted to be with him. As he lay in the hospital bed, hooked up to four different IV drips, I could see the various incisions on his torso. The first was for the assumed appendicitis, the second and longest, for the exploration of the abdominal cavity. The third, I never fully understood its purpose. From each of the incisions, tubes led to plastic Coke bottles on the floor, which were cut in half and used to collect his draining fluids. Walking through the hospital hallway, I noticed rubber gloves drying on the heaters, possibly for use a second or third or fourth time. There were no heart monitoring machines. There was nothing to assist with oxygen. Every now and then a doctor would come by, lifting up George's wrist to check his pulse.

Sitting down with nationally renowned surgeon Dr. Akramov, I noticed a variety of pictures on the walls of his office taken with famous people. Offering us tea, he was most cordial, knowledgeable, and generous with his time. Explaining and reexplaining the diagnosis and George's condition to us, Dr. Akramov also openly shared his frustrations as a medical professional working in such a corrupt, callous, and crooked environment. Himself educated in Kiev during the time of the Soviet Union, Dr. Akramov had managed to build up a variety of international connections over the years, even having traveled to the United States to participate in professional medical seminars. Himself a lover of music, Dr. Akramov was known to generously sponsor orchestra performances at the Kyrgyz National Opera and Ballet Theater.

Flying into Bishkek on that Sunday morning, Pam came directly to the hospital, spending the day by George's side and talking with the various doctors. Due to the generosity of someone in the States, buddy-passes on an airline were granted so that all of the children would be able to fly to Bishkek, whether from the States or Ukraine. One by one, the family began to arrive, and one by one each made the trek to the hospital. Rhonda came with her son, and spent almost every moment in the hospital with George. Having finished nursing school, Rhonda was able to understand much of what was happening, give a better explanation of the medications needed, and make up for what was lacking in terms of nursing care. During that time she observed a great deal. She shares, "I watched Mom and Dad talk a lot. Dad wept a lot at the end. He wept most when he heard how people were praying for him, when Mom would tell him that people had called or written. Those things touched his heart so much."

Over the next few days as each of his children would come into the room, George would speak words of blessing over them. Rhonda continues, "I remember Jonny coming in and Dad asking him about his music. He told him, 'Jon, you keep playing.'" Jon remembers when he first came to the hospital. He says, "It was hard because I had never seen Dad like that. I had never seen Dad as not being strong. He always seemed stronger than me, even as a grown man. But I remember walking into the hospital, and Mom said, 'Jonny is here.' Dad took the sheet and he covered his face, because he was crying. He didn't want me to see. That first time I saw him, he didn't say a whole lot. But then the second time when I came in, my music was playing on the CD player. Dad looked at me and said, 'Jonny, your music, it ministers to people.' He got really choked up and he couldn't talk, but then he continued, saying, 'And it's ministering to me.' I remember the doctor at the hospital loved classical music. He had a piano in his office and he wanted me to come play it. Somebody told Dad that I was going to go play the piano, and Dad said, 'Oh, go bless 'em.' That was kind of like my commission. 'Go bless 'em.' That was the last thing he said to me. When I was playing that piano, I remember Mom telling me that Dad had asked her if that was me playing. And she said yeah and he started crying again."

Little David was now 6'6", and taller than anyone else in the family. When he arrived at the hospital, his dad's condition was much worse than he had anticipated. David shares, "When I first saw him, I realized that things with Dad were much worse than I had even imagined. The condition of the hospital shocked me too. Even though I had grown up being in hospitals like that, I never had to be in one for very long. There are terrible things that you only realize when you have a loved one who is suffering and living in that condition. I remember asking God, 'Why? Why take my dad, who was a much greater light in this dark world than me?' Maybe that's why his death put a spark into me, and so many other people – because when he was gone, I felt like the world was going to miss out on that love that God was pouring through my dad as well as his simple faith and obedience to God's call."

David continues, "I don't remember him talking much in the hospital, but I do remember seeing the pain on his face. When I prayed for him, he would agree with me in prayer. He liked my massages and was always apologetic when I had to clean up after him. What I remember most is that he asked for me when I was not there, and when he was being put on the plane he asked where I was. It was one of the first times in my life when I felt that he needed me, and one of the few times that I felt like I was actually helping him."

When George Robert came in, his dad burst into tears, his firstborn son leaning over him in the bed. I remember standing at the door of his room as George's deep cry reverberated throughout the hallway. This post-operation period in the hospital in Bishkek was intensely painful for George. Any spoken sentences were short because of the pain. After the tears had passed, George spoke what would be his final exhortation to his son: "Give them the Word. Don't hold anything back. Let it fly." All of us took turns spending the night with George, assisting him, monitoring him, and gleaning as much information as possible from the doctors. It was difficult to find the necessary medicines, hours spent daily on the roads going from pharmacy to pharmacy. Since patients in the hospital are responsible for providing their own bedding, all soiled linens had to be driven home to be washed. Any meals had to be prepared and brought in for those spending the days and nights with George. It was becoming increasingly obvious that the care and monitoring after the surgery was severely insufficient. After praying and counseling with doctors in the States, Pam made the decision that it was time to pursue the option of medical evacuation to the States for George.

EVACUATION AND TREATMENT IN THE UNITED STATES

Without health insurance or a medical evacuation plan, we were at a loss as to how to pay the required six-figure amount for the plane trip back to the States. However, once again, the Lord provided as a pastor placed the entire cost of the evacuation on his credit card. Churches, friends, and loved ones, both in the States and around the world, then sent funds to help cover the costs of the evacuation.

Medical evacuations are not a quick procedure in all parts of the world, especially in Central Asia. After the decision had been made, it still took five days for flights plans, airspace permissions, landing rights, and so on, to be granted. On the day the plane and crew arrived, hopes were high for a quick evacuation of George. Yet once again, we were forced to wait as rules required them to rest for a certain number of hours. Renee shares, "We were trying to reassure Dad that they were coming. But then, once they got there and told us that we had to wait another day, we begged them to at least come to the hospital and see George to give him hope that it would be soon." As the German doctors entered the hospital, they told us that they were not allowed by international law to provide any kind of assistance to George until he was on their airplane. However, when they saw his status and the condition of the hospital and equipment, they began telling Rhonda and others items to move, which drips to redo, and what needed to be adjusted to keep him alive. They were not even permitted to hook up any oxygen to George, and they were visibly shocked at the conditions. "We are going to get you out of here, Mr. Markey," they said as they walked out of the room. In tears and taking the doctor's hand, George said, "Thank you." That visit and that statement helped George hang on for one more day.

Finally, the day came. The ambulance pulled into the hospital parking lot and George was carefully loaded inside. Following him in our cars, with an escort from the U.S. Embassy, we drove to the airport. As we waited for the plane to be prepared and for all the paperwork to be completed, each family member had the chance to step into the ambulance and say goodbye to George. Everyone was looking forward to his arrival in the States and hopeful for his recovery.

After the last leg of the overseas flight, the plane touched down on the tarmac at Indianapolis International Airport. My cousin, Steve Leach, was in charge of airport operations at that time, and had orchestrated all of the details for a smooth arrival. As the plane pulled into the terminal, the waiting ambulance drove up to meet the plane. Dr. Scott Murphy climbed out of the ambulance and remembers seeing George brought off the plane. He says, "It was so grim, just how weak George was. I remember they were monitoring his oxygen level, and it kept dipping down. I remember thinking, 'Is he even going to make it out of the airport and into the hospital?' He was sick, very sick. It was very cold and snowy." As the evacuation doctors collected their equipment, they soon realized that they had not taken George off of their gurney. Giving one last reminder of the differences between medical practices, the doctors laid George on the snowy asphalt so that they could get their gurney and blankets, the wind blowing over George as he lay on the icy ground, uttering "Cold, cold, cold."

Arriving at the Indiana University Medical Center, George was immediately given a complete examination and evaluation. Although somewhat crude, the operation in Bishkek had stopped the necrosis. However, as the results came back from the lab, it was determined that five forms of bacteria were growing in George's incisions. Even though the operation had helped stave off death, the poor sanitation and deplorable after-care conditions in the hospital had resulted in bacterial infection, venous collapse, and other physical traumas. As he was stabilized, David, Rhonda, and other family members began returning to the States and coming to see their dad in the hospital.

Soon, other people from all over the country began calling and even coming to visit with George in the hospital. Old friends like Mike and Lyn Abney from Crawfordsville and Joe and Susie Bruch from Portsmouth. Family, like George's sister Rhonda and her husband, Mike. It seemed that the Lord was giving people time with George, perhaps time that they had not had for years. Mike Abney remembers talking with George in the hospital, telling him, "I bet you're preparing a lot of sermons in your head." George replied, "Oh, if I were, they'd sure be different." One by one, people came by the hospital to visit, assist, and pray with George and Pam. Outpourings of love were lavished on George and Pam. Memories were shared of lives changed through the influence and example of George. For almost 10 days, George lay in the hospital, the doctors beginning to speak of recovery.

IN SICKNESS AND IN HEALTH

Sometime back in January while he had been in the States for the missions conference, George had managed to purchase a Valentine's Day card for Pam. Inside was written, "I thank God for you, my helper, my lover, my best friend. Today and every day, may you know how special you are and how much I love you. I am blessed that out of all the people in the world, the Lord chose you to be the perfect one for me." As the evacuation was being prepared, Renee found this card and placed it in Pam's bag to take to the States. Now in the States, with Valentine's Day approaching, George asked whether Pam had gotten his card. "Yes," she replied with a loving smile on her face. And in view of the approaching holiday, Pam had something special in mind to give to George. The doctors were beginning to speak of his recovery, and George was finally going to be permitted to eat. Pam decided to celebrate by making George some pink jello, in honor of the upcoming "day of love."

Theirs was a special relationship, one that had been made solid through years of caring, consideration, and commitment. Having lasted through the difficulties, endured days of difference, and grown through times of struggle, George and Pam had forged a relationship that was truly remarkable. Though they did not write any marriage books, always frank about their own insufficiencies, George and Pam provided an example of a passionate, dedicated love that left those around them with little doubt of their resolve. "I remember that Mom and Dad were always affectionate to each other in front of us kids," shares Renee. "It had a way of affirming to us that they were the only ones for each other, that they truly loved each other." Now, through card and jello, even in these tumultuous and painful days and weeks in the hospitals, George and Pam were showing each other love and tenderness.

THE FINAL DEPARTURE

Pam was holding George's hand when he began struggling for breath. Doctors immediately rushed in. Surrounding George, they began to work on him. Finally releasing George's hand as the medical staff proceeded to close in around him, Pam was escorted out into the hallway and then to a small room where she was joined by a priest to wait for any news. Pam Shares, "I heard the "code blue" from that room and wondered if it was for George. Soon the doctor came in and I asked him if they had resuscitated him. The doctor answered 'Not yet, but I'll let you know.' This answer was a blessed hope for me, if only for a few minutes. But it was only a few minutes later that he returned and gave me the news. My response to the doctor was 'but I thought he was getting better' and he said 'So did we.'" Doctors and nurses had been frantically working on George, but to no avail. A large blood clot had broken broke off and was lodged in between his heart and lungs. With no oxygenated blood circulating in his body, George's passing into eternity was quick. February 13, 2007.

Arriving to the hospital, Shani Williams, former missionary and family friend, quickly took over the place of the obviously relieved priest. Pam continues, "Before they let her onto the hospital floor, they had asked her if she were family, and she answered 'I am the closest thing she has to family right now,' just so that they would let her in to see me. I remember saying 'The Lord gives and the Lord takes away, blessed be the name of the Lord,' and then the piercing pain settled in. I remember walking down the corridor of the hospital to his room wondering why I didn't collapse. And then I was sitting by his body and feeling his absence, so acutely."

Pam continues, "I read everything that anyone gave to me in the days after he was gone, longing for any word that would ease the pain of separation. Of course the foundational comfort was Jesus, and all the other books and comments were built on that Divine Comforter. So many times I had read about people who had suffered loss and how that what others say to them is so inappropriate, seemingly unfeeling, not comforting. But I so longed for any word that would ease the pain, just to hear from others no matter what was said. I found their desire to share comforting. I remember writing in my journal, 'Come and grieve with me, come anyone, I am not selfish with my sorrow. There is enough for all.' What others said, even if it was a 'Praise the Lord, George is in a better place,' it didn't upset me because I wasn't struggling with anger at all, just profound sadness.

LETTING THE FAMILY KNOW

The phone call came at around 3:00 in the morning on February 14, our time in Bishkek, Kyrgyzstan. Valentine's Day. Awakened by the penetrating ring, and not waiting to arouse our one-month-old daughter, Rachel, I quickly reached for the phone. After a few hesitating seconds with no answer on the other line, I heard Pam's voice asking for Renee. Passing the phone to Renee, I knew the words that were going to be spoken from thousands of miles away. "Your daddy is in heaven." Beginning with the oldest, Pam had begun calling each of the children to inform them. As Renee put down the phone, all we could do was hold each other in bed, uncontrollably crying, heaving, sobbing. Not enough air. Perhaps it was only a dream. All that had been done to get him to the States. All of the prayers, support, phone calls.... Now he was gone.

THE TRIP BACK

With hopes high for George's recovery, we had not even considered making plans to return to the States. Furthermore, because we had not anticipated a return trip to the States so quickly after the move from Ukraine, there were no funds for one ticket, let alone six. As the body of Christ began to hear of the news of George's passing, churches and individuals began calling to express their sorrow and to make sure that we were planning to return for the funeral. Unsure. The decisive call came from the church in Kiev, the body there undergoing its own time of mourning. Upon hearing of our hesitancy to return, they immediately told us that they were sending us money to help with our tickets. More tears. A church that had been dependent on us for so long was now there when we needed them. The body of Christ around the world reaching out to provide much-needed comfort. True love.

Functioning on autopilot, we began to make plans to leave. But how could we travel without a passport for Rachel, who had been born there in Bishkek only a few weeks before? Calls and trips to the U.S. Embassy were immediately rewarded with a passport being issued in less than one day. The flight back to the States took us through Istanbul, Turkey. Awakened at 5:00 in the morning by the Muslim call to prayer, I lay in a hotel bed saddened by the cryptic, melancholy prayer as it rattled throughout the city's three thousand mosques.

Arriving in the U.S. during one of the worst snowstorms to hit the East Coast meant that our planned connecting flights were canceled, and no one knew for how long. Those in the States monitoring our travel began making alternative plans even before we landed. Calvary Chapel of Old Bridge, New Jersey, arranged two vans to pick up our families and drive us to Philadelphia, from where we could fly into Indianapolis in time for the funeral. They met us with bags of food and drinks, lovingly providing for any needs that we had. Those family members traveling from Ukraine had an even more difficult time with connections, cancellations, and delays, resulting in a much later arrival to the States even though they departed before we did.

Tim and Shani Williams, close friends and former missionaries, opened up their home to the entire family. Sporadic conversations, memories, and even laughter began to fill the rooms. A family picture was taken of us in the basement while all of us were still in our pajamas. The day before the funeral I asked Pam what George's last words were. She paused, seeming to have not even considered this herself, and then said, "'Jesus.' His last words were, 'Jesus, Jesus.'"

SECTION 3 PHOTOS

The Markey family in Ukraine in order of age: George, Pam, Renee, George Robert, Robin, Rhonda, Melanie, David, Jonathan, and Aaron, about 1997.

George and Pam riding the Kiev metro together.

Passionate times of prayer in a packed apartment.

Father and son George Robert baptizing together
at national conference, spring 2002.

A transformed son, Jonathan, embracing his father at a conference.

George answering questions with leaders at a conference.

The ordination of Alosha Satenko, future pastor of
Calvary Chapel of Kiev, spring 2003.

A time of worship among the churches at a national conference, spring 2003.

At David and Deborah Markey's wedding: all of the family together, June 2005.
Back row: Robin, George Robert, Jonathan, Renee, Rhonda.
Front row: Melanie, George, Kristen, David, Pam, Aaron.

Gourleys, Billings, and Markeys together in Bishkek, Kyrgyzstan, fall 2006.

EPILOGUE

ON THE DAY of the funeral, hundreds of dear friends and family members began arriving at Horizon Christian Fellowship in Indianapolis. In reality, it was a time of celebration, even though hearts were breaking and tears were being shed.

Pastor Bill Goodrich began, "This is the celebration of a wonderful man who has been in our lives and has affected each one of us. George was one of my very best friends, but he is up in heaven. He is seeing what we do not see right now. I am jealous. He always beat me to whatever it was."

After Pastor Phil Twente's opening prayer, Pastor Ed Gaines read the following eulogy: "George was all about pointing people to Jesus. George was a brother, a husband, a father, grandfather, pastor, friend, and much, much more. He lived a full and exemplary life, because his life was dedicated to pleasing and glorifying his Lord and Savior, Jesus Christ. George often said of himself, 'I am a rich man,' because of his wife, children, and grandchildren. God's work through George will continue to bear fruit many years all over the world. His joy in the Lord brought hope to and inspired many. He lived a revolutionary life, always full of energy and fiery love for the Lord. He was generous and a compassionate man. We will miss him greatly. But we know he is glad to be in heaven, the place he spoke about constantly as being his true home. He often said, 'When I die, this old dead body is not George Markey. George Markey has simply moved. My address has changed. My passport says I am an American, but my citizenship is in heaven. I am just passing through.' He kept a light touch on this world because he kept his eternal destination in view...

"And his desire was that his extended family, classmates, neighbors, and all with whom he came in contact would come to know Jesus Christ and experience His love for them. George fought the good fight, he finished the race, and kept the faith. There is laid up for him the crown of righteousness which the Lord will give on that Day, and to all who have loved and longed for Jesus' appearing. (II Tim. 4:7-8) Jesus said, 'I am the resurrection and the life. He who believes in me, though he may die, he shall live. And whoever lives and believes in Me shall never die. Do you believe this?' (John 11:25-26) And George would ask you this morning, 'Do you believe this?'"

John Chubik shared, "It is times like this that challenge us to think of the lessons that we have learned from these ones that God has placed in our lives. Our lives are not the same after we have known a George Markey. That God uses men like this. They are rare. They are special. And as our lives come in contact with their lives, we are changed by them, by Christ working through them. For George, to live was Christ. George was a pioneer. Pioneers are special people. They are people who are very often misunderstood, and perhaps unappreciated at certain times of their lives, because they are doing things that nobody else would do, or understand what needs to be done. They are the ones that strike out into new territory, and George was that kind of man. And to understand George, you had to understand that phrase 'to live is Christ.' It was the great motivation of his life in all that he did. In every move of George Markey's life, there was this motivation to be closer to Christ, to be more fruitful for Christ, and this was the thing that drew him and his family through life. As I watched the family function and make decisions in the ministry, this is what determined what was to be done. George courageously followed Jesus Christ. George was the real thing. A man sold out to Jesus Christ, every action, decision of his life. Everything speaks to that."

I was surprised when I heard George's voice coming over the speakers. It tore at my heart; it penetrated my being. They were playing a recording of one of his final messages he gave in Kiev, Ukraine, before leaving for Kyrgyzstan. In that message George shared, "He said to them, 'It doesn't matter whether I live or die, but that Christ be magnified in my body.' And the famous verse, 'For me to live is Christ, to die is gain.' And I don't know, my days are numbered – I am older. I have no idea when my departure from this earth will be. I've always thought that Jesus would come before I died. I believe he can come at any time. But maybe I will go be with the Lord first. I don't know. Why is it gain? Well, personally it is gain because that is our home. If you could just talk with anybody who has already gone to be with the Lord, if you could just have a conversation with them, they would say to you, 'Oh, you poor people. You don't know what you're missing. Why do you want to be down here? And you doctor your pains and you get old and can't hardly walk. Why do you want to live down there? It's awesome up here.' It wasn't very long ago my wife's dad, John Pemberton, went to be with the Lord. I am sure he has no regrets. His family wishes he were still here. He doesn't. He would say, 'Oh, I can't wait for you to join me up here.

It's awesome up here.' It gives me great hope because there is no hope in this world. And as time passes, you will see that. It is a good thing our hope is not here – it is in heaven with the Lord!

As his body was laid in the ground near his parents' graves in New Ross, Indiana, on that cold, snowy day, all of those whose lives had been touched by his life now had one more reason to long for heaven.

George Winston Markey, pulling up his tent pegs one final time, made his departure to be with the Lord. His longing was realized. His God, glorified. His life was, as Pastor Chuck Smith described, "a life of simple faith, simple trust in the Lord."

In a message that George once shared from Revelation, chapters 21-22, he says, "Today we are going to look into eternity. But how can you describe eternity? There really isn't any way, because we are creatures of time. When the Bible speaks of eternity, it is as though we are just as a flower that opens – we see its beauty, and then we die. Or, I think one of the best examples – have you ever seen a little kid blow these soap bubbles? They go out into the air and then all of a sudden they burst. Our lives on earth are like that, compared to eternity. But very soon we are going to be in eternity. And the question today is, where will you spend eternity?"

AFTERWORD

As of today, it has been seven years since George Markey went home to be with the Lord. One of George's favorite verses which he quoted often was, "Behold, children are a heritage from the Lord. The fruit of the womb is a reward. Like arrows in the hand of a warrior, so are the children of one's youth. Happy is the man who has his quiver full of them;" (Psalm 127: 3-5). George's legacy continues through his family, serving in many places throughout the world.

His beloved Pam continues to teach and model Christ to Bible college students as the director of the School of Missions at Calvary Chapel Bible College Europe in Vajta, Hungary, where she lives with Kristen. George Robert and Jon, and their families, continue to serve in church planting, currently in Ternopil, Ukraine. David and his family are working to establish a church among an unreached people group in northern Siberia. Paul and Melanie Billings, having turned over the work in Kyrgyzstan to national leaders, are pursuing possibilities among Muslim peoples in the Middle East. Also having left Kyrgyzstan, Renee and I are looking forward to the next season of our lives and ministries, prayerfully considering opportunities in church planting in the Caucasus region. Robin and Rhonda and their families continue to serve the Lord in the States, and are also preparing for and praying about opportunities in overseas missions. Aaron is completing his education at Kentucky Christian University, and spends his summers serving in Ukraine and Hungary. The 27 grandchildren are growing up hearing the many stories of a faithful God who did a great work through a man of simple faith and simple trust.

JED GOURLEY
February 13, 2014
Indianapolis, Indiana

"For our boasting is this: the testimony of our conscience that we conducted ourselves in the world in simplicity and godly sincerity, not with fleshly wisdom, but by the grace of God..."

II CORINTHIANS 1:12

ACKNOWLEDGEMENTS

THANK YOU to my family who has been so encouraging and supportive throughout this project. To Renee, the love of my life, my special treasure: thank you for your companionship in this adventure, as well as every other adventure we have had for the last 20 years. You are amazing! To Anna, Lizzy, Joshua, Rachel, and Isaiah: you are the biggest part of our ministry team—so helpful, joyful, friendly, kind, loving, and so much more. I am honored to be your father, and I look forward to seeing where the Lord is going to take each one of you.

Special thanks to Pam Markey, John Chubik, and Bill Goodrich for spurring me on in the writing of this story. Also thank you for the many hours of sharing your own stories, reading over the text of this one, and making constructive remarks and corrections.

Thank you Cheri Clark, for your labor in editing the manuscript, giving helpful comments, and being available. Also, to Angie Vanderburg, Kathy Gilbert, Cara Denny, and Felice Ip for taking out many "bumps in the road."

Thanks to the staff at the Crawfordsville Public Library for aiding in the research of this book when I was 6,500 miles away.

Many thanks for each one who shared your memories and photographs. Thank you for your own life examples as well.

AUTHOR'S NOTE: The reader may notice my use of the Russian transliterations of Ukrainian cities, names, and other words, instead of the more correct Ukrainian transliterations (for example, "Kiev" instead of "Kyiv"). I chose to use the Russian transliterations for ease of readability and because they are more widely known in the United States. Most U.S. media outlets continue to use Russian transliterations, rather than the more proper Ukrainian transliterations.

Get in touch with us at:

www.distantfields.com

contact@distantfields.com

Made in the USA
San Bernardino, CA
14 July 2014